D1232077

LAW WITHOUT ORDER

BERNARD LANDE COHEN

LAW WITHOUT ORDER

Capital Punishment and the Liberals

ARLINGTON HOUSE
New Rochelle, New York

FIRST PRINTING, SEPTEMBER 1970
SECOND PRINTING, APRIL 1971

Library of Congress Catalog Card Number 79-115347

ISBN 0-87000-097-7

MANUFACTURED IN THE UNITED STATES OF AMERICA

TO *Alyce, Richard, Susannah, Charles,* AND *Ariel*

Acknowledgments

For their services, I would like to thank the following libraries and their staffs: the Burbank, California, Public Library; the Fraser-Hickson Library, the McGill University Library, the McGill University School of Law Library, the Westmount Public Library, and the Young Men's Hebrew Association Library—all in Montreal; and the National Library and the Library of the Supreme Court of Canada—both in Ottawa.

For in a state that hath no dread of law
The laws can never prosper and prevail.
Where dread prevails and reverence withal
Believe me, there is safety, but the state
Where arrogance hath license and self-will
Though for a while, she run before the gale
Will in the end make shipwreck and be sunk.

—SOPHOCLES, in *Ajax*

Contents

LAW WITHOUT ORDER

Introduction

I have seen the deterioration of public morality and the loss of respect for the reign of law. These have impelled me to write about laws that have failed to bring order and rules of procedure that take little note of the violence of our times.

No one argues that public health matters are the exclusive province of the medical profession. And lawyers and judges are not the only accredited authorities on law and order. The average citizen, untrained though he may be in its intricacies, must look to the law as his one source of security. This alone entitles him to pass judgment on the law's strength and effectiveness. Admittedly, however, the thinking of men with specialized training and experience deserves prior recognition. Yet these men of professional expertise differ among themselves on the contentious matters hereafter dealt with. It is my privilege to draw upon their combined wisdom, and to examine their opinions, if not always with complete impartiality, at least with the deference to which they are entitled.

The concept of law, it has been observed, sprang from an innate sentiment for justice within the human heart.[1] This is a great truth. So implanted in human nature is the distinction between right and wrong that persons whose own conduct is less than satisfactory are invariably insistent that all others behave ethically. In the unchanging moral sentiments of the human heart the penal laws of all nations are anchored.

But what of the sanctions for breaking the laws whose fundamental sameness is everywhere discernible? It is in this area that some abysmal differences clamor for attention. A starting point is the unresolved issue of capital punishment. Though here and there triumphant, the movement for the total abolition of the death penalty has by no means been greeted with universal acceptance. Even within those jurisdictions where

[1]Mr. Justice James C. McRuer, *The Evolution of the Judicial Process,* Clarke-Irwin, Toronto, 1957.

the issue seems finally to have been settled, debate is lingering on. But only within the context of a much expanded inquiry, I would maintain, is further discussion likely to be fruitful.

CHAPTER 1

Critique of Anticapitalpunishmentism

THE MOVEMENT FOR MITIGATING THE HORRORS AND FREquency of the death penalty has a distinguished record. In our own time, its underlying motivation has become powerfully entrenched throughout the greater part of the free world. And yet in face of the acquired absolutism of this campaign, I challenge its dogmatic assumptions, whose logical imperfections are obvious. As an example of reasoning that is vulnerable, here is part of an address delivered by a member of the Canadian House of Commons: "I believe that the death penalty serves no purpose. Its champions argue that it is a deterrent to murder, and the police lobby and its spokesmen agree; but statistics and history show that it has no deterrent effect. The shots fired by a misfit named Harvey Oswald on November 22, 1963, knocked the rickety props out from under this favourite argument of the champions of the death penalty. Three presidents of the United States had been assassinated before John Fitzgerald Kennedy was shot down in Dallas. All their assassins died. . . . This did not deter Oswald."[1]

The sweeping and categorical assertion that "the death penalty serves no purpose" is contradicted by a number of self-

[1]From a speech by Reid Scott, M.P., during debate on a motion to abolish capital punishment, in the Canadian House of Commons, March 24, 1964.

evident facts. There is no shortage of reported instances wherein more than one homicide was committed by the same culprit, either as a result of not being apprehended on time, or after being erroneously acquitted, or during an escape from prison, or upon a fellow prisoner. This being so, it is at least incontrovertible that a killer, once he has been liquidated, is forever incapable of killing again. Considered under this aspect alone, it would seem that the death penalty has in the past achieved at least one purpose.

Additionally, it bears pointing out that since the time when the right of private justice was taken over by the state, grief-stricken relatives were in effect guaranteed that their cry for vengeance would be listened to. To high-minded persons, such a consideration might seem utterly unchivalrous. But inasmuch as we are duty-bound to take into account the sentiments of the many who have not been able to reach the higher levels of spirituality, the imposition of the death penalty for murder could assuage in some measure the feelings of those who have lost a husband, a father, or a son.

Still another demurrer could be entered to the dictum of the honorable member that the death penalty serves no purpose. But, it is a point that I bring up with some hesitation, out of deference to the proprieties. It has to do with money. To hang a man or to electrocute him entails less of a financial burden on the taxpayer than to board him as a prisoner even for a few years, let alone for the remainder of his lifetime. Consider also the fact that with the passing of the years, the character of the prison population is being increasingly tinctured by an ever rising infusion of more terrifying inmates. It is perhaps the too ready acceptance of the dogma that "the death penalty serves no purpose" that has helped to give rise to a situation in which the maintenance of discipline within prison walls becomes increasingly problematical, requires a more numerous staff, and, not least of all, places in jeopardy the lives and the morals of the rehabilitable element of the prison population.

The "police lobby," for which the member for Danforth apparently had little esteem, happens to represent on this issue the corps of qualified and experienced law enforcement officers of the entire Dominion; but no less so, according to all reports, their colleagues of Great Britain and the U.S.A. as well.[2] Since the opinion of these officers is entitled to such little respect, what other body of professional men, may it be asked, is deserving of any greater credence?

Criminal lawyers, it will be answered, are as a body very well informed as to the psychology of criminals and their friends, and so their views on matters concerning public safety ought to be listened to with great attention. To be sure, neither they nor the police can be credited with being objective and dispassionate on this important issue. By the very nature of his job, the policeman is not expected to think kindly of men in contact with whom he daily risks his life. Criminal lawyers, on the other hand, except those who serve as public prosecutors, are disposed to be more charitable towards an element with whom they enjoy a bread and butter relationship. Notwithstanding, even among defending attorneys there are not wanting those whose experience has led them to conclude that for murderers in general—always excepting their own clients—the death penalty ought to be maintained. One of England's most notable barristers, Sergeant Ballantyne, who in his book informs us that "few barristers have defended more accused persons than myself," was a strong upholder of the death penalty.[3] Likewise, the names of many eminent jurists could be cited as entertaining the same opinion.

Continuing with the claims put forward by the honorable member, it remains unclear why, among the many political murders of recent years, the assassination of President Kennedy should be viewed as being in some exceptional way responsible for having "knocked the rickety props out from under the favourite argument of the champions of the death penalty." "Three presidents of the United States," we are reminded," had been assassinated before John Fitzgerald

[2]For the attitude of the English police see P. J. Fitzgerald, *Criminal Law and Punishment,* Clarendon Press, London, 1962, p. 225.

[3]Sergeant Ballantyne, *Some Experiences of a Barrister's Life,* Richard Bentley, London, 1898.

Kennedy. . . . All their assassins died. . . . This did not deter Oswald."

Now a number of observations suggest themselves in reference to this convulsive interpretation of a shattering though not unprecedented episode. We are invited to enter with confidence into the shadowy realm of the subconscious, a realm where truth and logic tend to operate from concealed bunkers. One might perhaps skirt the question as to whether the assassin Oswald, here somewhat charitably referred to as a "misfit," was so historically minded as to be aware of the end of his murderous predecessors. History does indeed bear witness that no less than three presidents of the United States were struck down, with their killers in each instance apprehended and disposed of. But history in its wider and deeper aspect records a large number of such episodes. According to the *Columbia Encyclopedia,* there were in Europe and North America no less than nine hundred politically motivated murders in the course of two centuries. Why only as late as November 1963 did the wise men of the world discover the utter uselessness of the capital penalty? Why were these "rickety props" not disposed of when President Lincoln was killed or President McKinley? Or perhaps much earlier when the Duke of Buckingham was slain in the year 1627? Even by that time the thinking part of the world had already seen enough of political assassinations.

Granting that Oswald, contemplating the death of President Kennedy, was fully aware of the grim fate that had befallen earlier assassins, he might have been reassured nonetheless by the reflection that times had changed since these earlier episodes. He was entitled to believe, in the event of being caught, that he would have available to him a battery of the most skilled and able counselors, generously paid for by the American taxpayers. Great ingenuity would have been displayed in his behalf by these defenders in blocking at least some of the damaging evidence against him. Errors in protocol before the jury inadvertently or otherwise committed by prosecuting attorneys could have offered endless opportunities for postponements, appeals, new trials, and whatnot. A plea of insanity, almost routine in such instances, would have gained at least some measure of support from respected psychiatrists. Even on the remote possibility of the death penalty being inflicted, it could only have happened after many years, during which time Oswald would have continued to be an international celebrity. All the while, he would have been housed in a comfortable prison, provided with all the amenities, well fed, and with the best of medical care.

Continuing our intriguing exercise of entering into the thought processes of this killer, it could be safely surmised that in 1963, he was fully aware of the fact that in the United States the death penalty, though not erased from the statute books, had by that time become an empty threat. Any threat of punishment—be it death, imprisonment, fine, or chastisement at school—once recognized as mere bluff, obviously ceases to be a deterrent. The case of Oswald, to say nothing of those who since have followed in his footsteps, does in a sense bear out the assertion that the death penalty has turned into a "rickety prop." But has it always been thus? With utmost finality and assurance we are advised that "statistics and history show that it [the death penalty] has no deterrent effect."

Now history covers an enormous span of territory and length of time. The pretentiousness and sweep of a dogmatic assertion that history proves a certain negative are alone sufficient to render it suspect. History properly understood is a tissue of contradiction; and from its pages there may be culled data that can be used to prove or to disprove almost anything. Thus, history informs us that many a tyrannical and bloody-minded ruler succeeded in prolonging both his rule and his life for many years, despite the proximity of enemies who would have delighted in his downfall. Surrounded though they were by danger, such rulers ended their lives peacefully. Is it not a reasonable inference, from what we do know of the ferocious penalties then decreed, not only for the murder of a prince but even for its bare attempt, that the overhanging specter of a hideous death awaiting an assassin played at least some part in protecting the lives of these tyrants? The fine, nowadays, for a motorist driving his car through a red light is approximately twenty-five dollars. Notwithstanding, a great many motorists continue to pass through red lights. Are we to say that because of this disregard of the penalty on the part of many car owners that it is entirely ineffectual and should be abolished?

Again, the utter ineffectiveness of the death penalty is said to be proven statistically. Now statistics are by all means entitled to respect; but they are not an infallible guide and are not exempt from misinterpretation. We must have qualifying references in all instances when we hear about the number of murders within a given locality, as compared with that of another. We are informed, for example, that in the six states of the American union where the death penalty has been formally abrogated (since then increased to thirteen), the murder rate was 1.83 per 100,000 of the population, while in the forty-two other states which have not followed suit, the murder rate was 7.04, or almost four times as high.[4]

It would appear from this comparison that not only did the abolition of the death penalty fail to bring about any increase in the number of murders committed, but the reverse was actually true. Eliminate from the mind of the would-be killer the dread of himself being put to death and you will incline him to give up his intention to kill. Manifestly, this conclusion would be absurd. It would tax the ingenuity of the most agile psychologist to explain such a change of heart. The more likely explanation for the disparity of these ratios is that there is, always has been, and always will be, within the wide expanse of the North American continent some divergence in the degree of violence manifested by the population at large, depending perhaps on cultural background, economic conditions, and the mixture of rural and urban population. In those particular states where the problem of murder has been minimal, one could expect less opposition to the abolition of hanging or electrocution than in those states plagued by a high incidence of criminality.

[4]House of Commons debate, March 24, 1964.

Within this small minority of state legislatures that have seen fit to do away with all executions and in whose states the rate of murder collectively is so minimal, no hint is given as to any possible divergencies among them. Is the rate of 1.83 to 100,-000 uniformly applicable to each of them? The answer to this question could be revealing.

Again, the statistical references made by our parliamentary debaters do not go beyond distinguishing between two general groups, those states which have formally abolished the death penalty and those which have retained it. As regards the larger group, where the percentage of murders is said to be 7.04 per 100,000 of the population, would it not be possible to discover some few states among them where there is in fact a much lower percentage than the overall, a percentage even as low as that prevailing within the opposite group?

Still another caveat must be entered. In 1961 not more than 43 persons were executed in the U.S.A., or substantially less than one for each state. Hence, it would seem that the differentiation between the handful of states where the death penalty had been formally abrogated and the majority where it had not, was hardly momentous, since in any case an intended killer in any part of the country would realize that *de facto* the death penalty had become inoperative.

Above all, all comparisons as regards the number of murders committed are shaky for yet another reason. There is no longer an agreed definition of murder. In a recent trial before a court in Montreal, over what the presiding judge termed "a macabre affair," two brothers, both with criminal records, had lured a young woman into an automobile, driven her along an unfrequented road, dragged her out of the car, and shot six bullets into her. The verdict of the court was "manslaughter."[5] Obviously, in any compilation of figures concerning murders committed in Canada during the year 1967, this dreadful episode will not be counted.

In our soft-spoken age, the word "murder" has for the most part made way for such euphemisms as "manslaughter" and

[5] *Montreal Gazette,* April 30, 1968.

"felonious assault," or else murder that is murder, but only "noncapital." It is difficult to take issue with the remark attributed to Professor Mergen of Mainz University in Germany that nowadays only a layman is in a position to determine who is a murderer and what is murder.[6] In both England and Canada, as well as the United States, that which in the fifties was considered murder is no longer called that in the seventies. In a later chapter, the matter of statistics of murder along with lesser crime will again be considered.

ON JUDICIAL ERRORS

Those opposed to the death penalty frequently argue that there is always the possibility of some innocent person being destroyed either through malice or through error, and that to avoid such tragedies it were better that no one be executed. There are indeed countless instances on record of innocent persons being knowingly harried to their doom through hatreds begotten of religions and politics, as well as the machinations of private enemies. Often enough statesmen and judges have participated in such guilty affairs, to say nothing of mobs. Somewhat less scandalous are those instances in which persons of generally bad reputation have, as a result of unconcealed bias, been found guilty of acts that they were quite capable of committing, but did not commit. The controversial Sacco-Vanzetti case is a possible example. These men, whether actually guilty or not, as anarchists and revolutionaries, had made themselves generally reprehensible to the authorities.*

The likelihood of judicial error has been diminished enormously through the institution of courts of appeal in all criminal matters. Invariably a verdict of murder is subject to minute scrutiny through not one, but a series of appeals, and not infrequently by retrials. Stringent laws of evidence reduce still further the possibility of judicial miscarriage. The art of cross-examination skillfully used by able and experienced spe-

[6] *Der Spiegel,* Hamburg, August 12, 1968, p. 33.
*I have not carefully examined the circumstances of this case, and therefore hold no opinion on their actual guilt or innocence.

cialists in the art has itself made corrupt and perjured evidence more difficult than ever. Organized bodies of opinion, along with a vigilant press, stand in readiness to raise the alarm on any suspicion of judicial railroading. In 1918, a certain Tom Mooney was tried in San Francisco on the charge of having hurled a bomb that killed ten persons taking part in a Preparedness Day parade. He was condemned, it was claimed, on the strength of fabricated testimony introduced with the connivance of the prosecuting attorney. He was in the end rescued from the gallows as a result of an investigation carried out by the editor of a San Francisco newspaper. Newspapers have been charged from time to time with hindering the cause of defendants in criminal prosecutions by what is often considered to be improper publicity. But by the same token can it be said of them that they have been vigilant in uncovering baseless prosecutions, and are certainly likely to do so in the future.

To the earlier sciences of ballistics and fingerprints have been added the subsequent triumphs of what is known as forensic medicine, to make even less likely the prospect of judicial error. "There are those who say that corpses don't talk, but indeed they do. They talk of easy living in pleasant homes, of hard dirty lives, joys that ended in sorrow, of tragedy, broken hearts, stupidity, cruelty, depravity, perversion, crimes of every kind."[7] Through the unceasing growth of medical knowledge devoted to studying the after effects of criminal acts, as well as by the harnessing of chemical analysis and atomic science, giant strides have been made in the refinement of laboratory techniques in postmortem examinations, all adding to an ever increasing confidence in the guilt or innocence of accused persons.[8]

That a vast number of prosecutions will continue to leave in their wake a strong element of doubt and of unsatisfied suspicion cannot be gainsaid. Indeed, a trial by its very nature is meant to distinguish between that which is certain and that

[7]Molly Lefebure, *Evidence for the Crown*, William Heinemann, London, 1955, p. 2.
[8]For details of such scientific advances, see Prof. John Glaister, *Final Diagnosis*, Hutchinson of London, 1964.

which remains conjectural. In by far the greater number of acquittals, the accused is discharged and freed, not on being certified innocent and utterly harmless, but only because the charge against him has not been proven beyond all reasonable doubt. It should be remembered that in law a basic principle, never contested in the free world, states that wherever any doubt remains, it is always the accused who is entitled to benefit from such doubt. The number of possible criminals so released is legion; and if they are not released in the first instance, they are so on appeal. So strictly is the principle of doubt interpreted in their favor that even persons with long criminal records are availing themselves of it. And often enough when we speak of doubt, it is one that requires an uncommon amount of skepticism to be maintained.

All this being so, it remains to be stated that not all court proceedings necessarily leave in their wake even a slight residue of uncertainty. To convert into a universal principle a legitimate lack of assurance that could be the outcome of many a court proceeding, and to maintain that such ambiguity is in every instance inevitable, would soon reduce to chaos the entire administration of justice.

Often enough the charge against the accused is easily substantiated, the testimony of the prosecution's witnesses fully corroborated, and all contradictory evidence conspicuous by its absence. Should under such circumstances a person be found guilty of murder and duly executed, there is not even the remotest possibility of a judicial error. Also, very often in cases of murder, the actual killing, as well as all its attendant circumstances, not only remains uncontradicted, but is freely admitted in open court or in some other fashion not subject to rejection. The trial may then pivot not on the facts but upon the motive. In more and more instances, the issue is not the killing, which is readily admitted, but whether or not the killer is insane. Should the weight of testimony indicate the absence of insanity, and the man be executed, again there could be no possibility of error as to the facts.

It should be pointed out, however, and this cannot be too

strongly maintained, that there is not a single human enterprise or sphere of activity that is not marred at some time by a deplorable episode. And yet no field of economic or other activity is inhibited by such possibilities. We do not, for example, cry out against the erection of tall buildings and bridges, or the excavation of tunnels, because invariably a certain number of persons lose their lives in the course of these undertakings. In the construction industry in the Montreal area, 69 men were killed on the job during 1966 and 45 during 1967. Injuries during this period varied from 6,621 to 8,150 annually. There has been no demand from any quarter that by reason of innocent men losing their lives, no further building should take place.

Acts of justice decreed by courts of law, and designed to punish persons who have made themselves enemies of their fellow men, will conceivably be marred from time to time by some tragic blunder. But unless these become flagrant and conceived in malice, one may continue in the hope that they will be held in check and minimized so far as is humanly possible. In any event, errors that result in the condemnation of innocent persons, tragic though they undoubtedly are, will likely remain insignificant as compared with blunders at the opposite pole. Loss of innocent lives could be the consequence, direct or indirect, of a thoughtless extension of what is sometimes all too frivolously referred to as "reasonable doubt" in favor of known psychopaths and infamous persons. Such an instance, and its baleful consequences, is recited by Professor Glaister, and is worthy of mention as only one of an innumerable category.[9] In the opinion of Professor Glaister, who as an expert witness testified on behalf of the Crown in a case involving John Donald Merret on the charge of murdering his mother, the accused was erroneously acquitted by a majority vote of an Edinburgh jury. This happened early in the twentieth century. Some twenty-eight years later, this same man had to be hunted down for the killing of two women. He would

[9]For a detailed description, see John Glaister, *Final Diagnosis*, p. 46 *et seq.*

undoubtedly have been found guilty had he not taken his own life as he was about to be apprehended.

Much is made of the comparatively remote possibility of some innocent person being hanged for a crime he did not commit. And yet hardly any note is ever taken of the lethal aftermath that can follow an erroneous acquittal. It is a false and utterly unattainable ideal of perfect justice and unerring accuracy that would sacrifice a hundred real and present advantages to society through the permanent removal of men who are really no better than noxious animals, in order to obviate the possible infliction of a wrong upon some unknown person at some unknown future date. This is almost like saying that society should be deprived of the use of electricity, because someone now and again is liable to be electrocuted, or that motor vehicles should be banned by reason of the large number of deaths on the highways. It is ironical that when known killers are liberated, no similar fears are voiced as to the possible consequences to some innocent persons, as yet unknown. With great complacency, the chairman of Canada's Parole Board announced recently that of 119 convicted murderers who since 1920 have been given paroles, a mere 9 percent had to be returned to prison, and among these repeaters was "only one" murder.

LIFE IMPRISONMENT VERSUS CAPITAL PUNISHMENT

The argument that a sentence of perpetual imprisonment is the most effective penalty for all antisocial actions was advanced long ago before the Roman Senate while sitting in judgment upon a troublemaker named Cataline.[10] Beccaria urged that for all major offenses, life imprisonment was a more severe infliction than death. Beccaria's reasoning was undeniably persuasive, given the prevailing conditions of prison life and its attendant tribulations portrayed by him with some vividness. However, leaving out of account the fate of prisoners in Mus-

[10]Sallust, *De Conjurationis Catalinae.*

lim and Communist lands, prisons such as Beccaria describes no longer exist. It should be remembered that he wrote his celebrated thesis several decades before the Englishman John Howard pleaded successfully for prison reform. The prisons of today, particularly those on this continent, with their excellent fare, their provision for entertainment of their guests, their medical services, and their friendly and assiduous array of psychologists and psychiatrists, constitute no formidable deterrent to most wrongdoers, certainly not to hardened and experienced postgraduates in crime.[11]

The eminent English barrister and defender of criminals, Sergeant Ballantyne, writing towards the end of the last century and at a time when prisons were very far from being the penitential arbors which they are in the process of becoming, was strongly of the opinion that for dangerous criminals, prison terms, however lengthy, were an insufficient restraint; and for murder, an inadequate substitute for the death penalty.

> When transportation was in force, it created much dread in the minds of criminals. There was a mystery attendant upon it, and a sense of final separation from every home tie. It operated also most strongly upon their friends and accomplices, thus creating what is most to be desired, an efficient example to others. Now their friends know where they are; and in the miserable holes in which they themselves grovel, in cold, starvation, and wretchedness, they are apt almost to envy the food and warmth of a prison. The crimes that are now creating a feeling allied to terror in the public mind are those which subject our fellow creatures to death or cruel injury, and the question requires very grave consideration, and a freedom from morbid sentimentality. . . . I have no doubt that there is no example of a criminal under a capital sentence who would not with joy exchange the penalty for any other punishment known to law.[12]

Undoubtedly, the dread of a lengthy incarceration even in a comfortable prison can be said to carry at least some weight;

[11]For example, see the report in the *Montreal Star*, January 10, 1969, on Britain's newest prison nicknamed the Ritz.
[12]Ballantyne, *op. cit.*

but in practice nowadays very few such sentences are of long duration. The imprisonment of a mother found guilty of killing her child can be counted on as being hardly more than seven years.[13] Prisoners prior to their trials have been heard to exclaim theatrically that rather than undergo permanent confinement, death would be preferable to them. Nonetheless, comparatively few so-called lifers are ever known to commit suicide. Hardly a day passes in which we do not read in our newspapers about defending attorneys resorting to every conceivable stratagem, both before and after their clients' conviction, attempting to save them from the gallows. Nor does the condemned man fail to be greatly relieved when informed that his sentence has been changed to one of detention for life. It is impossible to avoid the conclusion that the forfeit most of all dreaded by careerists in crime is also the one that offers the greatest possible discouragement to those who might be inclined to follow in their footsteps.

Altogether aside from its admonitory function, however, the supreme penalty has yet another merit to recommend it. The mere incarceration of a dangerous killer at best offers to the society from which he is ostensibly removed only a partial security. On the North American continent, walking out of a jail or prison is almost as common as walking out of a restaurant. Most likely to abscond, having undoubtedly the greatest incentive to try it, is the convicted murderer whose sentence has been generously commuted.[14] Even should he fail to escape or regain his freedom by other means, the "lifer" remains a constant menace to the other inmates of the prison, to say nothing of its officials and guards. It is superfluous to demonstrate, on the other hand, that under the terms of a well-timed execution, once a killer never more a killer.

[13]According to the findings of a twenty-five-year survey conducted by the Lafayette Clinic of Detroit, a high though indeterminate percentage of deaths among children, supposedly accidental, are actually unproven cases of murder committed by their parents, chiefly mothers (*Jewish Daily Forward,* New York, September 1, 1968).

[14]"Three convicts, one serving a sentence for murder, escaped from police cells, the murderer having been reprieved by act of the Federal Cabinet in 1966" (*Montreal Gazette,* May 1, 1968).

IS THE DEATH PENALTY IMMORAL?

In a book written by a former governor of the state of Ohio, the immorality of taking the life of a murderer by the state is strongly affirmed.[15] "Punishment," we are told in his Introduction, "is too often a matter of emotion rather than cold logic." The author's preference for the latter is of course implied.

Now as an example of the author's adherence to "cold logic," the following passage is revealing. "No one who has ever watched the clock marking the last minutes of a condemned man's existence knowing that he alone has the temporary God-like power to stop the clock can realize the agony of deciding an appeal for clemency." The comment could here be made that some degree of compassion ought to go out to a man in public office faced with the necessity from time to time of making a decision of some difficulty. However, a plea for changing the law in order to relieve him from such a quandary is entitled to no respect whatever. Unless, of course, it can be maintained that the duties devolving upon an officeholder ought invariably to be pleasant and decorous. The fact that in the process of enforcing a law someone in authority is compelled to spend a number of sleepless nights should be a matter of complete indifference to the public that has chosen him for the job.

For the governor of a state in the United States or for a solicitor general of Canada to have to decide whether or not a sentence of death should be carried out is perhaps an abrasive experience. Yet, on the whole, less so than for other officials concerned in the matter. To apprehend the killer and bring him to justice could have been a dangerous undertaking for the officers of the law. For the prosecuting attorney, with any kind of humane feeling, the asking for a death sentence was likewise no easy matter, nor for the judge and jurymen who handed down the sentence.

To proceed further with the tract of Governor DiSale. "Dur-

[15] Michael V. DiSale, *The Power of Life or Death*, Random House, New York, 1965.

ing my term as governor," he goes on to say, "I came to dread the days leading to an execution." But apparently on no more than twelve occasions during his entire tenure of office was he called upon either to confirm or to reverse a court decree of execution; and over a period of years for a territory as large and populous as the state of Ohio, this was not too excruciating an experience. Out of this number, he informs us, in exactly one half there were justifiable grounds for reprieve. As a conscientious public servant, however, sworn to carry out the law, regardless of his private reservations, he did permit the remainder of the condemned men to suffer their fate, commenting, "I could find no extenuating circumstance, no unequal justice, no questionable legal procedure, no reasonable doubts to justify my reversing the sentence of the courts."

Now we are here faced with an admitted distinction between two categories of convicted persons. We need have no quarrel with a decision of the governor waiving the death penalty where it seemed to him proper to do so; and we are to assume that as a public officer both honest and conscientious he used his discretion wisely. To argue, however, that were it not for a severe and unjust law, the same indulgence ought to have been shown to a class of killers manifestly distinguished from those who did merit pity, is to advocate a morality that mocks at justice.

Let us examine further the new ethics of this revisionist statesman. "I believe that taking a human life even to pay for a human life already taken is immoral. I am not speaking of morality in an abstract theological sense, but in a personal sense." We are invited to contemplate a new revelation, admittedly at variance with all traditional views of right and wrong. We are in effect being invited not only to change the penal laws as enunciated in the law books, but to embrace a fresh moral outlook, in which what at one time was considered right, is now to be considered wrong, and what at one time was considered a crime deserving of the severest punishment, is now to be treated as no more than a regrettable aberration. In the name of this allegedly higher morality the repeated Biblical injunctions regarding the doing away of murderers are to be ignored.

Under this revolutionary code of ethics, it must be assumed that it is a matter of indifference as to how many killings were perpetrated by the murderer. His life under all and any circumstances remains sacred. Nor does it matter, if we are to be consistent, whether the act of murder was in peace or in war.

Shortly after the outbreak of the Second World War, the English passenger liner *Jervis Castle* was sunk by a German submarine with a loss of several hundred lives. The sinking was traced to information furnished to the enemy by a spy. The spy was tried and found guilty and hanged. Presumably, under the new "personal" morality of Governor DiSale, such a punishment was quite uncalled for.

THE STATE MAY NOT KILL

A well-known publicist living in England, in a book written in condemnation of capital punishment, rhetorically wishes to know why governments whose purpose supposedly is to deter people from killing one another should themselves consider it necessary to indulge in "legalized killing."[16] He then proceeds with his own answer. The reason for this is popular ignorance, deliberately fostered by reactionary politicians, judges, and officials. A more matter-of-fact reason could be offered, however.

The state has a duty to protect itself and its citizens not only from foreign enemies, but from the domestic variety as well. There are occasions when to forestall anarchy and chaos, the choice is between killing or being killed. This will not be disputed, even by the most confirmed ideologues. But further, in any civilized state, be it "reactionary" or not, the lives of innocent persons are no longer wantonly taken away. Only in the case of the most unforgivable crimes is there a question of forfeiture of life.

Admittedly, the right of a government to take the life of any

[16]Arthur Koestler, *Reflections on Hanging*, Gollancz, London, 1956.

of its subjects ought to be subject to the strictest review in all instances. I would add that no matter how deserving of death an offender might be, and how little deserving of any pity, it would be entirely wrong to inflict any torture upon him, or any form of death that is of an exceptionally painful nature. The infliction of the death penalty for such transgressions as theft, smuggling, currency violations, black market activities, counterfeiting, and seditious remarks—as is common practice behind the Iron Curtain—is utterly reprehensible. Yet in protest against such inhumanity, we need not jump unthinkingly to the opposite extreme, by proclaiming it a categorical imperative that no crime, however, dastardly, is deserving of death.

If we are to talk in terms of what is morally right or wrong, can it not be asserted that it is the paramount duty of the state, undeterred by obfuscations about "rights," "vengeance," "eye for an eye," and similar verbal roadblocks, to offer to its citizens the utmost in protection, in the light of all known experience, from killers, sane and insane, actual and potential?

If a state seeks to place itself on the side of the moral law and to acquire respect for itself and for its laws, we expect a plurality of virtues, but without yielding to extremist opinions. The ethical state must refrain from deceitful practices, in dealings both with its own citizens and with strangers. It must remain true to all its promises, whether of a commercial or a political nature. It must remain faithful to its allies even at the price of temporary inconveniences.

But such a state must be strong as well as virtuous. And for strength there may often be a requirement for adequate harshness, severity, and even brutality. It must put aside both unnecessary cruelty and ill-advised leniency. Not only is it permissible for the state at times to take the lives of its internal enemies, but there are occasions when, by failing to do so, it becomes responsible for the insecurity of its own citizens. To deny the state the moral right to take the life of anyone becomes all the more bizarre and unrealistic in view of the as yet undisputed right of one individual to take the life of another under given circumstances. Now, let us imagine a situation, hypothetical and yet not improbable, in which you find yourself threatened by a gunman. You happen to carry a loaded weapon under a valid license from the authorities, and making effective use of it, you kill the marauder. Obviously, under the existing law, no charge will be laid against you, once the facts have been verified in your favor. You might even meet with the congratulations of some of your high-minded and liberal friends, regardless of the fact that you have taken the life of a human being.

Now, continuing the illustration along the same vein, let us imagine a less happy outcome of the encounter. Your assailant is faster on the draw so that you are the victim. The courts, following some of the recent guidelines as to what is murder and what is something else, could conceivably decide to call it noncapital murder, second degree murder, manslaughter, or felonious assault. But let us assume that they would be so old-fashioned as to term it murder, pure and simple. Now, according to the enlightened ethic of those who would obliterate the capital penalty, such is the sanctity of human life that the killer's right to go on living must under no circumstances be denied him; all the more so, since by the time the matter has come to a head before judge and jury, the homicidal act in question will have lost much of its shocking impact. The votaries of this ultra-charitable cult are readily enough moved to repugnance by ugly deeds, but their indignation subsides very quickly. They are, in the words of a contemporary author, people "who would forgive everything bad, even forget it . . . like Lady Anne in Shakespeare's *Richard III.* Their wrath is short-lived, their will not steadfast, their memory weak."[17] These "bleeding hearts," as they are sometimes designated, have two logical difficulties to contend with. To begin with, why is it proper on occasion for a private citizen to take the life of another, while the state may do so under no circumstances whatsoever? Again, if it is allowable to deprive a would-be murderer of his life, in order to forestall his attack, why is it

[17]Alexander Solzhenitsyn, *The First Circle,* Bantam Books, New York, 1969, p. 30.

wrong to take away his life after he has successfully carried out his dastardly business? The answer is to be found in the realm of psychology, rather than in those areas of morals and logic.

The surrealist notion, originating in India, that in no instances is the taking of life permissible, is rapidly developing into a liberal dogma. For example, it is no longer permissible for the police to shoot anyone "merely" in defense of property rights.[18] Proposals to put down riots and arson and looting by shooting when other means of prevention have failed the police, have been rejected by most governors and mayors on the ground that "life is more important than property."

In the state of Israel, there has been until now no death penalty for murder. It is known, however, that nearly eighty percent of the population is in favor of introducing the death penalty for Arab terrorists who plant bombs and dynamite. Through political necessity, this movement has thus far been resisted by the Israel government. To hang even a single Arab guilty of terrorism would invite a storm of protest that would reverberate from one end of the globe to another and would endanger the precarious sympathy for Israel in its struggle with the Communo-Muslim world. However, there is hardly any outcry—outside the United Nations, that is—when the Israel Air Force raids a camp of guerrillas, innocently rubbing the sleep out of their eyes, or peaceably sipping their morning coffee, and kills those whom no tribunal has found guilty of anything. There follows a general shrugging of the shoulders, as if to say that these brave fellows simply had to take their chances. An attentive view of the matter would perhaps suggest that what is reprobated by "world opinion" is not so much the taking of human life in general, as the taking of life in an orderly manner, and under the judicial observance of forms. Otherwise expressed, it is not so much the infliction of death that is objected to, as the manner in which it is done. To the imagination, hanging impresses itself as being more ghastly and frightening than shooting. You may shoot a man so long as

[18] *U.S. News and World Report,* May 13, 1968, p. 42.

you have him on the run; but once you have captured him, you may not hang him or electrocute him—the objection being that "such extreme measures brutalize a society which is already too brutal. It adds violence to a society which is already too violent."[19] The observation of the distinguished president is specious and nonsensical. A report that a well-publicized killer has met with his just deserts will not "brutalize" in any further degree those who read the newspapers, listen to the radio, and watch television.

I offer the following quotation as illustrative of the emotionalism with which the entire thesis of anticapitalpunishmentism is impregnated. "The nation state exacts its pound of flesh in the name of justice and calls it freedom. Read in this sense ancient history presents one vast charnel house. For one of his circuses, Claudius had 19,000 condemned 'criminals' brought home to be killed in the public games. . . . Among the victims were thousands of helpless individuals, freemen and slaves, accused of no crime at all; but on their bones the unsteady throne of the Caesars rose a few inches higher."[20] Now the warmheartedness of this indignant recall of ancient wickedness can't be disagreed with. But there is no connection whatsoever between the mass victimization of their fellow creatures by monsters, such as Claudius, and the problem of how to deal with yesterday's thug who poured gasoline over an old woman and then killed her by setting her on fire. For doing what is necessary to combat a wave of contemporary murder, the doleful recital of ancient or even twentieth century holocausts contributes nothing constructive.

THE SACREDNESS OF LIFE

According to the latest doctrine of liberal-minded churchmen, life being a Divine gift, it is the Creator alone, and not the state, whose privilege it is to deprive anyone of it. Such being

[19]Morris B. Abrams, president of Brandeis University, as quoted by the *Montreal Star*, October 21, 1968.

[20]James Avery Joyce, *The Right to Life, A World View of Capital Punishment*, Gollancz, London, 1962.

the case, the question arises whether the state has the right to impose even a lesser punishment, such as imprisonment. Since the murderer will in the course of time meet with Divine justice, is it proper that he should be penalized twice for the same offense? The Creator, it is conceded, does indeed take the lives of his creatures by a variety of means. He frequently does so in the hecatombs of warfare, by epidemics, and by accidents of many different kinds. But why, may we ask, does the Creator not choose to do so through the instrumentality of the police, of duly constituted courts of law, and of state-appointed executioners?

On May 22, 1968, in Kiel, Germany, a former Nazi, S. S. Major Friedrich Schmidt-Schuette, was sentenced to two years imprisonment for having on March 29, 1944, ordered the execution of no less than seventy-three airmen of the Royal Air Force who were recaptured by the Germans while attempting to escape.[21] The report went on to say that the four other members of the German execution squad for these airmen had been sentenced to death by a British military court in 1945 and immediately hanged. Schmidt-Schuette, the principal culprit, was apprehended only years later. To assert that the German court which in 1968 handed down its mawkish sentence was acting in accordance with God's will is sheer blasphemy. The "Divine gift" argument, carried to its logical extreme, would provide a refuge for every marauder who might threaten you with a gun or knife; or who might threaten to rape your wife, burn down your barn, or loot your merchandise. To deprive such a being of his "Divine gift" would automatically transform into a transgressor every intended victim who defends too strenuously either his safety or his possessions. After all, should anyone point a gun at you, what right have you to decide that he is actually a sinner? You are not in the place of God. In any event, you are not to assume that he really intends to pull the trigger. Even if he does, the shot need not kill you. And for a mere wounding, you do not take a man's life. If you come upon

[21] *Montreal Star,* May 22, 1968.

him as he is about to set fire to your store, or if he should attempt to hold you up, it is only a matter involving property; and what are material possessions compared with the life of an errant brother? The goods that he is about to deprive you of, you will surely regain after a few short years of further toil. "Who steals my purse steals trash," a great poet once taught us to believe. Such is the sacredness of human life, we are informed, that under no circumstances may anyone be deprived of his portion thereof, not on account of having committed a villainous act, and certainly not over any question involving material possessions. In a sense, it is to be conceded that the lives of all sentient beings are sacred, and not only those of human beings. But sacred, or not sacred, there are times when life must be sacrificed or taken away. It should be noted that this doctrine of the sanctity of human life was enunciated a very long time ago, though not to the point of absurdity, when it was declared, "Whoso sheddeth man's blood, by man shall his blood be shed: for in the image of God made he man" (Genesis 9:6).

Undeniably, the deliberate and ceremonial taking of the life of any member of the human race ought to be offensive to the feelings of a civilized and humane person; and this is the reason that for nearly a century executions have not been performed in public. Nor, it should be added, is the public at large encouraged to view the day-to-day holocausts carried out inside our abattoirs and slaughterhouses. Nevertheless, that which is aesthetically repugnant to our senses may on occasion have to be endured. A society already well inured through press and other media to acts of violence and bloodshed, both actual and fictitious, could reasonably be expected to endure with some composure the tale of an occasional and well-deserved execution.

The execution of a murderer nowadays, on such rare occasions as it still occurs, be it on this continent or in some far-off place, such as Rhodesia, gives rise to a bout of international hysteria infinitely more affecting than any indignation that might have followed the perpetration of the crime itself. It is now customary, in fact, to equate an execution for a crime with the crime itself, and to consider one as wicked as the other. The late Clarence Darrow, pleading before the court on behalf of the killers Leopold and Loeb, asserted that the taking of the lives of these men by the state would be a crime even greater than that which they committed.[22]

By a host of well-meaning advocates, clergymen, politicians, and social workers we are assured repeatedly that the taking of a man's life by the state, for whatever cause, is "immoral." This word comes quite easily to those who will go on pretending that we are living among the lotus eaters. William F. Buckley Jr., in his book *Up from Liberalism,* speaks of the present-day passion for the muted expression. We soften our meaning by speaking of exceptional children, when we really mean backward children; of "emerging nations," when we are really referring to those that are uncivilized; of people who are "idealistic," when we really want to say that they are muddle-headed. So it is with reference to killers. They are referred to nowadays as "disturbed persons" or "lonely figures." However, there is likewise present the opposite tendency, that of calling a spade, not a spade, but a steamshovel. Hence some refer to the taking of the life of a convicted killer as "immoral" when they ought really to content themselves with calling it distasteful.

Obviously, the hanging of a criminal, no matter how hideous his crime, is an unpleasant and repulsive business. All taking of life, not only human but animal as well, and under all conceivable circumstances, is an awesome process. No person nowadays, with any pretense to decency of feeling, would care to be present at an execution. Nor, for that matter, would he relish the spectacle of his protein food being prepared inside a slaughterhouse. Nevertheless, we do not, because of our own sensitivity and good breeding, brand as villainous and inhuman those of our fellow citizens who are called upon to perform such necessary acts.

[22]Arthur Weinberg, *Clarence Darrow, Attorney for the Damned,* Simon & Schuster, New York, 1957.

ON VENGEANCE

Under the masochistic morality of our time, severity in dealing with those guilty of bloodshed is stigmatized as "revenge," and this is looked upon as a greater crime—or at least as great—than the motivating offense. The alleged sinfulness of revenge, vengeance, or retribution—call it what name you will—has never been established. There is no text to be found in Holy Writ that condemns, without reservation, the "passion for revenge." We are indeed commanded, "Thou shalt not avenge, nor bear any grudge against the children of thy people" (Leviticus 19:18), and further on it is written in the name of the Lord, "To me belongeth vengeance and recompense" (Deuteronomy 32:35). The reconciliation of these two texts presents no particular difficulty. The first of these exhortations is intended to surmount standing blood feuds and implacable animosities between individuals and families. The individual who has been wronged by his neighbor is forbidden to execute his own justice. But to denounce as "vengeful" or "punitive" the punishment decreed by a court of law of a heinous offense, in instances where guilt has been amply proven, is mere prating.

There are those who seem to think that evil deeds ought to be resented, but not punished, or at least never punished to the extent that the law provides for. The most recently evolved moral doctrine to the effect that hatred and vengeance are invariably wicked in themselves is in contradiction of the plain and unalterable facts of life, and is unsupported by any arguments deserving of serious attention. Love and hatred, recompense for benefits received and vengeance in some form for injuries sustained, are everlastingly opposite sides of the same coin; and in no society is it possible to maintain one in the absence of the other. The unqualified manner in which the desire for retribution is currently denounced by many politicians, clergymen, and philosophers is in itself proof that this sentiment is deeply planted in human nature. No doubt it is often subject to perversion, and has on many occasions been displayed far in excess of what is just and desirable. But in our own overcivilized milieu, the problem is now that too many people are accepting acts of violence and cruelty, deliberate fraud, and lawless turbulence with all too little response in the way of anger.

> The sentiment of just vengeance or retribution is too deeply grounded in human nature, and embodied in too many religious and moral codes, to be thus lightly dismissed. It is profoundly foolish to suppose that anyone can by the free use of ugly epithets, eradicate the desire to return a blow or to give active expression to the resentment against injury. It is not only barbaric people who regard punishment as a duty.... It is one thing to attempt to impose limitations on the brutality of natural vengeance. To attempt to preach it out of existence is sentimental foolishness.... If the natural desire for vengeance is not met and satisfied by the orderly procedure of the criminal law, we shall revert to the more bloody vengeance of the feud and vendetta.[23]

In what manner, can it be asked, does "the primitive passion for revenge" differ from what might with equal aptness be called "the primitive passion for justice"? That which is primitive can be good as well as bad. For a mob to break open the doors of a prison and proceed to hang an accused person who has not even been tried is both primitive and barbarous. But the capacity of men and women to be horrified by a murderous assault, and to demand adequate justice, though it too may be labelled primitive, is not any more reprehensible than the equally primitive passion for eating a good meal, or for making love.

"We should give equal, if not prior consideration, to the teaching of the New Testament rather than conform to the Old Testament. If Christ's admonition to turn the other cheek . . . has any real meaning, it categorically rejects the barbaric practice of retribution."[24] Now there is nothing wrong with this doctrine of turning the other cheek, in the case of those who

[23]Morris R. Cohen, *Reason and Law*, Collier Books, New York, 1961, pp. 52, 54.
[24]J. A. Byrne, M.P., House of Commons debate on capital punishment, March 23, 1966.

choose to live by it. But, it is a wrong doctrine if we seek to impose it upon those who, by nature and circumstances, will have none of it. And to the legislator who urges that this moral precept be converted into an act of Parliament, the following question could be asked: Whose cheek is it that you are so ready to turn to the hand of the smiter; is it your own cheek or those of other people? Shall we admonish a distracted widow, crying out for the law's vengeance, as follows: There, there, now, you must not be so vindictive. We are living in the twentieth century, don't you know? This poor devil just didn't know any better. After all, it was only a murder. He might commit an act of treason during the next war. Now that, of course, would be a hanging matter.

That we are living in the supercivilized twentieth century is indeed a fact. Unfortunately, the fellow with the gun does not seem to know one century from another.

There is yet another aspect of this question that I cannot forbear to mention. By substituting a sentence of life imprisonment for the penalty of death, do we really cease being primitive and revengeful? Keeping a man behind prison walls from his youth until his dying day in extreme old age, and depriving him, during forty or fifty years, of the joys and pleasures of normal living, is hardly a light punishment, though less drastic than sending him to the electric chair or the gallows. If, in answer to this objection, it is said that in practice such a person would not serve an entire lifetime, but would likely be released after only a few years, then we are confronted with still another dilemma. In Canada, between the years 1957 and 1967, there was not a single execution, even though it was still called for in all cases of capital murder. The fact cannot be dissembled that what has since been accomplished, in effect, is the removal of one penalty that did not do what it said, in favor of another that is equally meaningless. Where, one might ask, is the improvement in the law's credibility?

AN EYE FOR AN EYE

By a tiresome reiteration of the shibboleth "eye for an eye," nothing is argued and nothing is proven. The full Biblical text ought to be recalled. It reads as follows: "And if any mischief follow, then shalt thou give life for life, eye for eye, tooth for tooth, wound for wound, stripe for stripe. And if a man smite the eye of his servant, or the eye of his maid, that it perish, he shall let him go free for his eye's sake. And if he smite out his manservant's tooth, or his maidservant's tooth, he shall let him go free for his tooth's sake" (Exodus 21:23–27).

Now it will be noticed that any relevance to be found in this material to the issue of capital punishment is confined to the very beginning of the passage. However, you will not arouse a great deal of emotion in behalf of a convicted killer by merely relating his doom to the injunction of giving a life for a life. But as a psychological tour de force, you will make his fate seem far more ominous by conjuring up the seemingly more dreadful if inapplicable portion of the text, and by pointing to what is remembered but no longer countenanced in a refined society.

Considering the times, there was nothing especially horrendous in such penalties. They were severe, but they did not go beyond the gravity of the offense. For the youthful ruffian who delighted in inflicting pain on those weaker than himself and unable to fight back, the punishment was a wound for a wound, a tooth for a tooth, or a stripe for a stripe, as the case required. For one who tossed a vitriolic substance into another's face, it was an eye for an eye. Should we look carefully into any of the written codes of past ages we are certain to discover prescriptions that are far more shocking to our sense of decency. To many a Eurasian and Afro-Asian dignitary, sitting in judgment, the penalty of an eye for an eye seemed far too gentle. If it came to blinding, it was not one eye, but both. King Henry VIII, the "Defender of the Faith," once ordered the right hand of one of his courtiers to be cut off for slapping his opponent during a tennis game.

For a long time now, the execution of criminals has had

nothing to do with their eyes or teeth, or any form of mutilation or torture whatsoever. "There is no doubt," writes an authority on the subject, a lady whose occupation it was for a number of years to assist at autopsies of executed criminals, "that judicial hanging compared with many natural deaths is merciful. There is no strangling. The combination of noose and drop jerks the head from the trunk and everything is over in a second or two. No one need have any doubt of the swift efficiency with which hanging is practised in our prisons to-day."[25]

CAPITAL PUNISHMENT AND THE POOR

Another of the grounds frequently urged in favor of abolishing the death penalty is that those upon whom it has been practiced were almost without exception poor and friendless.[26] A warden of Sing Sing prison was quoted as saying that of the hundred and forty-nine prisoners whom he personally had escorted to the gallows, not one among them had any money. Parenthetically, it could be suggested that these hundred and forty-nine had reached a stage in their careers when having money or not having it did not matter a great deal. Also, in the circumstances in which they found themselves, being broke could be regarded as perfectly normal, considering the assumption that their lawyers had spared no efforts in their behalf. It bears emphasizing, moreover, that being poor, in the absence of other mitigating circumstances, is no ground whatever for being treated with more leniency than one who is not poor. As for being friendless, this is a condition that is not necessarily brought on by poverty. Friendlessness, particularly in a convicted murderer, could also be induced by a lack of amiable qualities.

Distinctions of this nature could be easily overplayed and oversimplified. Within a free and prosperous society, the exact dividing line between the rich and the poor is impossible to draw, as both concepts are subject to an almost infinite number of variables. Admittedly, this difficulty is somewhat lessened

[25]Lefebure, *op. cit.*, p. 78.
[26]House of Commons debates, March 24, 1964.

when it comes to distinguishing between the tenants of a prison. Since affluent convicts are conspicuous by their rarity, it could be reasonably asserted that nowhere does the ideal of equality approach realization so much as inside the walls of a prison. The question of opulent candidates for the death chamber doing better than their insolvent brethren is nowadays purely academic. When executions were still in vogue, there could have been hardly any doubt that the son of an industrialist or political leader, finding himself in any such peril, would manage somehow or other to soften the hard heart of justice. Without disputing this probability, it is to be conceded that among those classed as underprivileged there were many reprieves likewise. Instances abound in which indigent men have been able to arouse a degree of sympathy and moral support that more than compensated for their lack of funds.

The privileged treatment accorded to well-capitalized malefactors lay not altogether in the supposedly uneven carrying out of death sentences. Persons well favored by fortune have not been often tempted to engage in criminal adventures that could place in jeopardy their very lives. This perhaps more than favoritism accounted for the fact that in the days of capital punishment none but "the poor and friendless" found himself in the shadow of the gallows. This is not to underestimate, however, the role of wealth and social position in helping to turn the wheels of justice. Let it be granted that the conviction for any crime at all, of an executive, a professional man, or a politician, is presently an uphill, nay almost hopeless, task awaiting any state prosecutor. It should be added, however, that on an equal footing with criminally disposed tycoons there stand an even greater number of accused persons who, though neither rich nor influential, are likewise very well sheltered from the stormier blasts of the law. These are the protégés of powerful and well-financed bodies, such as underworld gangs, trade unions, the Communist party, as well as all those who for one reason or another have won the sympathy of welfare organizations like the American Civil Liberties Union and the National Association for the Advancement of Colored People.

A poor man, with an ample defense fund placed at the disposal of his lawyers by some concerned organization, or even the United States government itself, enjoys every advantage available to the son of a rich family and perhaps then some. Hence, when we talk about the social and economic aspects of a criminal trial—be it for murder or some lesser offense—the terms "rich" and "poor" may only be used with reservation.

Mammon, among his numerous aptitudes and talents, is an excellent advocate. In a court of law, his services are available to rich defendants as a matter of course. But to an even greater extent, to a much larger group among the nonrich as well. If you have enough money, you can engage for your defense as many as three of the best and most experienced lawyers available. Without money, you will have to get along with one solitary beginner. More appeals, motions, and objections will be entered on your behalf, when you are being served, not by a lone, underpaid, and disheartened practitioner, but by an amply subsidized battery. But this is not all. With enough money, you can persuade a sufficient number of professors of psychology to forsake their comfortable offices, come to visit you in your cell, and later on swear on the witness stand that at the time of the shooting, you were either insane or at least in a bad frame of mind.

CAPITAL PUNISHMENT AS A DETERRENT

Is the death penalty an effective deterrent to murder? The answer which I propose to give is both in the affirmative and in the negative. I have endeavored to point out that for society to give full expression to its abhorrence of murderous deeds is in itself a laudable objective. But it also remains largely sterile, unless it has the effect of a salutary warning to others. A penalization that is so tepid and halfhearted as to amount virtually to an act of forgiveness, can scarcely be conceded as having any deterrent value. On the other hand, a system that is so vicious as to take no account of moral restraint, will in the end almost certainly fail of its purpose. Unfettered cruelty by governments will undoubtedly have some disciplinary effect for the time being; but will surely end up in plots, uprisings, and revolts in which sporadic acts of criminality occurring within a relatively peaceable society will only give way to mass carnage and destruction.

Within the contemporary world, perhaps the outstanding example of an extreme faith in the efficacy of punishment as a deterrent is Soviet Russia. Crime statistics are a state secret.[27] Berman has estimated, basing his findings on newspaper accounts of individual trials, that between May 1961 and May 1962 there were in the Soviet Union about 250 executions. Between the latter date and the end of the same year, a period of seven or eight months, he estimated an equal or perhaps greater number. Considering the terrorist nature of the regime, and the fact that virtually all serious crimes carry the death penalty, it is not unlikely that the number of executions has since been accelerated, to say nothing of imprisonments and deportations, which in some instances are in their practical outcome almost the equivalent of death sentences. The closing feature of, this cycle will perhaps not be long in coming.

Those who, at the other extreme, repeatedly and dogmatically assert that the death penalty is no deterrent either to murder or to any other crime, are themselves the product of a rigid and unswerving doctrine. They would have us believe that in all instances when evil thoughts intrude into the minds of men, inhibitory fears play no part, and to the extent that they just might, the fear of death by execution is not among them.

Obviously, the prospect of an untimely end does not impress every human being in the same way and to the same extent. In the case of killings which are politically motivated, and which form a fairly large category, belief that a meritorious act is being performed often is sufficient to outweigh all fear of the consequences to the killer's own person. The urge to martyrdom has in similar fashion impelled many a crime in further-

[27]Harold J. Berman, *Justice in the U.S.S.R.*, Harvard University Press, Cambridge, Mass., 1963, p. 86.

ance of some religious principle. On a descending scale of motivation, the desire for booty and unearned possessions has at all times propelled many persons of little conscience to an all-out risk. The fear of a disgraceful and ignominious death is certainly greater in some than in others. Age is an important factor, youth being more thoughtless and reckless of consequences. Sex, too, is a determining factor, with women being generally far less addicted to violence than men. State of health counts for something. Persons of robust health respond to a challenge differently from those habitually given to imaginary as well as real fears of the future. Education, or lack of it, and other elements of refinement enter into the thought processes. Whenever a crime is committed on impulse, fear of the consequences will be more readily forgotten than in instances when some deliberation has taken place. Those reformers who profess to be so certain that the specter of the gallows or the electric chair or the guillotine at no time plays any part in the reflections of those about to embark upon a heinous adventure are in effect proclaiming that they have an insight into the soul of each and every killer and would-be killer.

For the death penalty to be always a deterrent would be truly remarkable. If the fear of the executioner were to become the uppermost factor in the minds of every criminal adventurer, there would perhaps be a cessation of all murder. But by the same token, the fear of an untimely death would equally bring to an end a large category of activities that are unquestionably lawful and proper. No one would then think of joining the army or the police force, or the fire-fighting force. There would be likewise a sudden stoppage of automobile racing, mountain climbing, stunt flying, acrobatics, hunting, parachute jumping, working on bridges, performing at circuses, detonating of explosives, and a host of other occupations and pastimes judged more than normally hazardous. However, the number of persons everywhere willing to assume these risks, be it for the sake of a livelihood, from recklessness, or pride, or devotion to some cause, is presently considerable. It is equally certain, however, that there are even more people who refrain from participating in these activities mainly because risking their lives is not to their taste.

In the United Kingdom, the Royal Commission on Capital Punishment, appointed in 1953 to examine the question of the deterrent value of the death penalty, reported, "We can number its failures, but we cannot number its successes."[28] In the subsequent debate in the Parliament of Great Britain, one member of the House testified that he at one time had contemplated a murder but that he had been swayed from his purpose by fear of the death penalty.[29]

No statistics are available, nor indeed any other kind of recordings as to the number and variety of murders that are perhaps being daily considered but not proceeded with, as to the instances of wives or husbands giving some thought to doing away with their spouses, but who refrain from so doing; or of businessmen into whose minds the thought might enter of getting rid of a detested partner or competitor by lethal means, but who resist the temptation of doing so; or of some householder who plagued by a disagreeable neighbor would love to see him dead and might at certain moments nourish the thought of inducing such a death, only to dismiss such a notion. Neither are any statistics available as to the number of professional and habitual housebreakers who, despite lengthy careers in crime, fail to carry with them any weapons in the course of their occupations. In all such instances, where the commission of a mortal offense is refrained from, there is obviously some inhibiting factor. Nonetheless, we are invited to believe that in no such instances, and they are perhaps legion, does the fear of the gallows enter into the thinking of would-be culprits. An assertion of such uncompromising eccentricity is a denial of common sense in favor of intellectual occultism and intuition.

We hear it argued from time to time that in the days when executions were an everyday occurrence, crime was nonetheless rampant. Despite the cruel penalties inflicted on those

[28]Cmnd. 8932, p. 20.
[29]House of Commons Debates, vol. 548, col. 2600, February 16, 1956.

who were caught, men were known to plot against the government, to ambush and kill bailiffs on the roads, to rifle the pockets of travelling bishops, and to consort with royal daughters-in-law. There have been gamblers in every generation. There are no means at our disposal for being able to separate those whom you can frighten from those whom nothing will frighten. But at a time when masses of human beings resembled beasts of the field in their readiness to indulge in combat and rapine, it would be interesting to speculate on what would have happened to the societies of that time had the extravagant penal laws suddenly become benign and easygoing.

The deterrent effect of the fearsome penalties of those earlier centuries was in all probability great; but by no means great enough. Poverty was crushing and all-pervasive, so that the fondness for life was diminished. Opportunities for learning an honest trade were minimal, while at the same time the opportunities offered by a life of crime were tempting enough. The primitive roads, travelled by foot or horseback, were an invitation to bandits and highwaymen. There were hardly any policemen, and their methods of detection were rudimentary. Escape was nearly always a fairly simple matter at the time when Europe was divided into a host of narrow jurisdictions, with extradition laws entirely unheard of.

"The main strength and force of a law," wrote Blackstone, "consists in the penalty attached to it." To be sure, there is not a single penalty attached to any kind of law that does not fail of its purpose in numerous instances. There are motorists who speed their automobiles in defiance of penalties; but it has not yet been suggested that such penalties have become useless and should be done away with. Such penalties as are provided against rapine and acts of violence and theft and forgery are often disregarded, of course; but this in itself does not prove that they are altogether ineffectual.

The dread of the gallows may have lost all its deterrent value, as many clergymen and politicians and lawyers solemnly assure us; yet, no one will deny that the rare hanging, which still occurs nowadays, does have a formidable impact, even if we judge only by the hysteria which it engenders and by the demonstrations of protest. It would be safe to conclude that if the impression is so shattering upon the guiltless, it must at the very least create some discomfort in the minds of the lawless as well. The theory that all violent men without exception are indifferent to the punishment of the gallows or the electric chair is to be rejected by the common observations of mankind. "And those that remain shall hear, and fear, and shall henceforth commit no more any such evil in the midst of thee" (Deuteronomy 19:20). Perhaps in our own time, persons harboring dark designs are more sophisticated than those to whom Moses refers. Perhaps their conjectures are different and there is no more fear in them; but it remains true, nonetheless, that having committed a crime, they still shrink from detection and arrest.

It can perhaps be asserted that while the would-be killer may be armed by a morbid insensitivity to crime and to its repercussion, he is known to lose his indifference once he has been apprehended and condemned. The Russian novelist, Dostoyevsky, in his famous work *Crime and Punishment,* set out to prove that a man's main punishment comes not so much from the fear of man-made justice as from the sense of inner guilt. And yet, in an earlier version of his celebrated work, he is known to have made the penetrating observation that "the proximity of punishment gives rise to real repentance in the criminal and sometimes arouses remorse in the most hardened heart."[30]

[30]Feodor M. Dostoyevsky, *Crime and Punishment,* Penguin Classics, p. 11.

CHAPTER 2

Capital Punishment: Its Growth and Decline

ANTICAPITALPUNISHMENTARIANS ENGAGE IN MUCH HISTORICAL retrospection, believing that an adequate knowledge of the past is essential for a wise understanding of the present. There are grounds for remarking, nonetheless, that a head saturated with historical data is not necessarily more adequately equipped for thinking clearly on contemporary events. Considered among the so-called humanities, history is perhaps the most engaging study of them all, providing as it does a zestful hors d'oeuvre to the events of our time. History is replete with many a fascinating report, nearly all of them true, or approximately so. Yet nearly always these recordings fall short of conveying the entire truth, their source material being regrettably circumscribed and deficient. Hence, a mere acquaintanceship with the annals of the past cannot of itself be expected to "unlock creative social forces."

Bearing this in mind, I have sought to avoid the error of using any of the episodes referred to in the present chapter, as a means of fortifying my previous or later arguments. History can rarely be safely used for building a case, human nature being such that even a scrupulous investigator will not always resist the temptation of leaving unmentioned facts that are both relevant to his subject and yet embarrassing to his thesis. As regards the specific remedy of capital punishment, to mention but one, I hold it impossible by any appeal to history to prove that it is either good or bad, effective or ineffective.

All this being so, I hold this historical part of my theme to be of some value, if only to indicate that all studies relating to the destiny of the penal laws must grapple with paradoxes and inconsistencies. Also, in considering the ebb and flow of institutions, history and chronology are often found to be at variance. The extensive tableau of the past is one of foreshortening and omitting, retracing and interlocking, with the orderly division of time into years and centuries being of diminished importance.

It is possible to affirm that efforts by governments to lessen private crime have, throughout the ages, oscillated back and forth between severity and mildness. Of many primitive nations has it been reported that their laws and customs were very far from prescribing the death penalty or indeed any severe punishments. Indicative of this attitude is the Biblical story of Cain killing his brother Abel. Cain is reproached for his deed; but quite foreign to the mind of the primitive annalist is the thought of any judgment to make the killer pay with his life.

"That which the murderer in Homeric times had to dread was not public prosecution, but the personal vengeance of kinsmen and friends of the deceased."[1] Some infusion of legality shows up, nonetheless, which in effect was designed to appease the relatives of the victim and, at the same time, spare the life of the killer. In cases where victims were persons of inferior status, payment of a given measure of beans was deemed to be a sufficient reparation. Herodotus reported that the Delphians belatedly accepted responsibility for the murder of the fabulist Aesop, who was a slave, and that they absolved themselves to everybody's satisfaction by paying a certain measure of silver to the grandson of the slave's master.

Among the early Germanic tribes, the sentence of death was inflicted mainly for theft, adultery, and treason. For murder or

[1]Grote, *History of Greece,* Collier, New York, 1899, vol. 2, p. 97.

other bodily injuries, monetary compensation was the rule and was known as *wergeld.* The amount of compensation varied according to the rank of the offender, as well as that of the victim. The type of weapon used was also taken into account. Killing another with an iron weapon was held to be less dastardly than shortening his life by clubbing him with a piece of wood, or working him over with one's bare hands. In bodily injuries, every limb and every imaginable wound had its established price.[2]

The reliance on propitiatory payment is well illustrated by an extract from the *Lex Salica* of the Frankish invaders of Gaul. "If three men carry off a freeborn girl, they shall be compelled to pay thirty shillings. If any person strikes another person on the head so that the brain appears, and the three bones which lie above the brain shall project, he shall be sentenced to pay thirty shillings. If it shall be between the ribs or in the stomach, so that the wound appears and reaches to the entrails, he shall pay thirty shillings besides five shillings for the physician's pay. If anyone steals a suckling pig and it be proved against him, he shall pay three shillings." Among some American Indians, the penalty of murder was the payment of a stated quantity of wampum to the heirs.

Now it seems on the face of it remarkable that among peoples normally violently disposed, their penal laws should have been so easygoing, even by present-day standards.

This seems paradoxical, yet is explainable nonetheless. In those forceful societies, a person with a grievance was permitted to help himself to all the justice to which he deemed himself entitled. But, as time went on, it became apparent that in practice this privilege of self-help was largely illusory. The predatory and insolent fellow who stole his neighbor's cattle and also carried off his daughter was likely to be too strong to be tampered with, by reason of his greater physical prowess, or his wealth, or the number of his friends and retainers. In cases of homicide, the so-called avenger of blood might only

[2]Menzel, *History of Germany,* trans. Mrs. George Horrocks, Collier, New York, 1900, vol. 1, p. 42.

be adding the forfeit of his own life were he to attempt to exercise his prerogative of private justice. In one of the Homeric passages there is depicted the utter helplessness of an orphan boy who, being despoiled of his inheritance, finds himself abandoned by his father's friends, whom he supplicates in vain and who harshly cast him off.[3]

It is not to be assumed, of course, that the system of monetary penalties for murder or assault was altogether without value. In an age of extreme penury, the payment of the required indemnity could be no light matter. The bereaved family, on the other hand, might often find itself sufficiently compensated for the loss of a member who in his lifetime was of no particular value to it. In any event, the poor fellow might have been robbed of his life in many other ways. He might have perished in battle or in an epidemic. In a crude sort of way, justice had been done. There was, to be sure, one drawback, and a very serious one it often turned out to be. Against a homicidal debtor, who was either unwilling or impecunious, some difficulty of collection could always be anticipated. Homer mentions an incident outside the gates of Troy, wherein one Greek slays another Greek hero in the course of some disagreement, and then dutifully deposits the required two gold pieces by way of reparation. Two sorrowing but equally grasping relatives of the victim reach out for the money, each crying out that his bereavement is the greater. To head off a possible crisis, the High Command deems it prudent to let the army as a whole decide the matter.[4]

The eventual disavowal of blood money as a means of justice and the substitution of the death penalty would in the parlance of our own time have been designated as "progressive." In historical Athens, some centuries after the heroic age, the law had been completely altered. Monetary compensation for murder was no longer acceptable; sentence of death was the unvarying penalty. Moses, a contemporary of Agamemnon and Ulysses, decreed, ". . . ye shall take no satisfaction for the life

[3]Homer *Iliad* 22. 487–500.
[4]*Ibid.*, 18. 497.

of a murderer, which is guilty of death: but he shall be surely put to death" (Numbers 35:31). In Ireland, monetary compensation for homicide was the customary practice as late as the sixteenth century. Much earlier, St. Patrick was said to have attempted, in the name of Christianity, to introduce the death penalty, but without success.[5]

The laws of the early Hebrews were distinguished from those of their neighbors by their severity in all cases of violence to the person. No allowance was made for age, sex, or social status. Exceptions were made for neither priests nor Levites, for neither rich nor poor. All homicides, with the sole exception of those committed accidentally, were punishable by death, no recognition being given to any distinction between murder and manslaughter, or between various kinds of killing.[6] The treatment meted out to ruffians whose misdeeds fell short of actual killing, was likewise less than kindly. For blinding, maiming, or wounding, mutilation was the general rule, so ordained as to tally with the offense committed. Other crimes—including adultery, homosexuality, sodomy, witchcraft, idolatry, kidnapping, and bearing false witness in capital cases—were also punishable by death.[7]

The laws of the ancient Hebrews were peculiar, since they themselves were a peculiar nation. We gather from their Scriptures that they were a people of mixed origin. They were descended racially, and to some extent culturally, from Babylonians, Canaanites, to a lesser extent from Egyptians, and possibly from Hittites, all such forebears being the most advanced nations of the Middle East. Notwithstanding, an aversion to the customs and practices of their Semitic and Egyptian kinfolk lay at the root of ancient Hebrew legislation. They were severe where these others were tolerant, and merciful where the others were cruel.

[5]John H. Wigmore, *A Panorama of the World's Legal Systems,* West Publishing Co., St. Paul, Minn., vol. 2, p. 705.

[6]Genesis 9:6; Exodus 21:14; Leviticus 24:17; Numbers 35:30, 31; Deuteronomy 19:11, 20.

[7]Four methods of the death penalty were practiced in ancient Israel: stoning, burning, strangling, and slaying wth the sword (see *Order of Service for the Day of Atonement,* trans. Reverend Dr. Moses Gaster, London, p. 187).

In the laws of Moses, sternness and compassion were intertwined. Theft was punished neither by death nor by mutilation. All capital charges had to be proven by the testimony of more than one witness. No accused person was tortured in order to have him confess, since such confession would have been invalid. In a later period, the Jews, while assenting to all that was merciful in their laws, sought to tone down those rules that they considered to be harsh and barbaric. The Pharisees, who came to be the dominant party, and who were the liberals of their days—in contrast to their aristocratic opponents the Sadducees—abolished the rule of "a tooth for a tooth and an eye for an eye," but they went much further. So stringently did they interpret the Mosaic requirement of two witnesses to a capital accusation, that the imposition of a death sentence became only a remote possibility. The seeds of the modern controversy over capital punishment were sown at that time. "A Sanhedrin [High Court of Justice] which puts to death one person in seven years is called bloody. Rabbi Eliezer ben Azariah says, if it puts to death one person in seventy years. Rabbi Tarfon and Rabbi Akiba both claim if they had been in the Sanhedrin nobody would ever be put to death. Whereupon Rabban Simon, the son of Gamaliel, retorts, 'The men who talk in this way multiply the shedders of blood in Israel.' "[8]

Within the Greco-Roman world, there was in all likelihood less application of the death penalty than in Western Europe as late as the eighteenth century. Slaves and other noncitizens were probably the main targets. The state could not afford many executions at times when all available freemen were needed for carrying on war. The archaic Law of the Twelve Tables included such ordinances as, "No one is to make a disturbance at night under pain of death"; "Libels and insulting songs are to be punished by death."[9] Murder was punishable by death, while theft was not. In the early period of the Roman Republic, murder in most instances was no longer punishable by death. But in a later period, when the triumph of

[8]Mishna Makkot 1:10, quoted from *Jewish Encyclopedia*, vol. 1, p. 170.
[9]Ortolan, *Explications Historiques des Instituts*, Paris, 1818, 1:114–180.

Roman arms came to be assured and the hoarding of manpower was no longer a problem, some heed was given to the clamor over deteriorating morals. Under the famous *Lex Cornelia de Veneficiis et Sicariis,* passed in the first century before Christ at the behest of the dictator Sulla, murder was once again punishable by death, but only in instances when it was the result of either poisoning or stabbing. The dagger was a lethal instrument not commonly found in the possession of an honest legionnaire, but was much made use of by less respectable characters. Poisoning was a method of destruction not infrequently chosen by the intriguing females of that emancipated era.[10] Some centuries later, in the reign of the Emperor Diocletian, seemingly by way of afterthought, this pivotal law was made applicable to the murder of one's parents, by whatever means. The capital penalty was likewise extended to take in robbers, incendiaries, and astrologers. The astrologers, being specialists in foretelling changes in the personnel of government, were none too popular with the establishment.

It would be highly erroneous to suppose that in the antique world judicially ordered killings were necessarily guided or restricted by written laws. Professional full-time judges were entirely unknown. Accused persons were taken before the ruler himself, or before a local governor, military commander, proconsul, prefect, mayor, provost, or some other person in authority. His discretion in such matters was all but unlimited. None of the written laws of antiquity that history has taken note of was actually known to more than a small segment of literati; those who might have been informed were not as a rule mindful of the laws. At the time of Emperor Caracalla, the average provincial magistrate probably knew less about Roman jurisprudence than a country lawyer in the Province of Quebec some eighteen centuries later. So limited in fact was the actual scope of the celebrated Roman law that its study was at all times restricted to no more than a few cities within the far-flung empire. There were in fact long intervals during

[10]Under the English Homicide Act of 1957, killing by means of poison was not included as capital murder.

which it was altogether forgotten even at Rome and Constantinople.[11]

Under the later Roman law, as reformed by Emperor Justinian, who announced himself as being "guided by humanity, common sense and public utility," bodily mutilation was instituted for nearly all crimes. Sentence of death was retained only for inexpiable crimes as, for example, in the case of the servant girl who happened to expectorate from an upper-story window at the very moment when underneath the body of Empress Eudoxia was on its way from the palace to the sepulchre. The spittle of this unmannerly wench scored a direct hit on the imperial sarcophagus. She was immediately taken care of by the state executioner.[12]

> The punishments in criminal cases were either fines and confiscation of property or mutilation. The death penalty after Leo III (717–740) was reserved for treason, desertion to the enemy, surrender, and unnatural vice, and even so was seldom carried out. Under John II (1118–1143), it was never once employed. Mutilation was considered a humane substitute, and was justified by the words of Christ about plucking out offending eyes and cutting off offending limbs.... We are apt nowadays to think it a revoltingly barbarous custom, but the fact remains that most people preferred, and still prefer, mutilation to death.[13]

Possibly most people do; but there were, even then, different ways of looking at the matter. In an age of extreme isolation and lack of communication, merely to dispose of an offender's life in a publicized manner was a warning to others not likely to travel very far. Depriving the offender of a lip, an ear, or his nose would serve as a more effective and lasting exhibition of the law's majesty. One might conjecture, on the other hand, that the presence of a multitude of defaced but far from impotent malcontents in the vicinity of the imperial palace could fuel a good deal of resentment for a regime generally reputed

[11] Steven Runciman, *Byzantine Civilization,* World Publishing Co., New York, pp. 64–65.
[12] *Ibid.,* pp. 56, 62–63.
[13] *Ibid.,* p. 86.

to be far from strong. Throughout the long history of the Byzantine Empire, the populace of its capital city was noted for its turbulence and riotousness.

Elsewhere, and throughout the centuries, the death penalty has had a checkered career, having been instituted and abolished and modified a great many times. The Buddhist rulers of India did not believe in the infliction of death for any reason and substituted for it fines, imprisonment, and mutilation.[14] In Anglo-Saxon England, the penalty for treason was on several occasions changed back and forth between death and mutilation.[15] The law of King Canute laid down as follows: "Though anyone sin and deeply foredo himself, let the correction be regulated so that it be becoming before God and tolerable before the world. . . . And we command that Christian men be not on any account for altogether too little condemned to death; but rather let gentle punishments be decreed for the benefit of the people; and let not be destroyed for little God's handywork, and His own purchase which he dearly bought."

The "gentle punishments" were as follows: "That his hands be cut off, or his feet, or both, according as the deed may be. And if he have wrought yet greater wrong, then let his eyes be put out, and his nose, and his ears, and his upper lip be cut off, or let him be scalped; whichever of these shall counsel whose duty is to counsel thereupon, so that punishment be inflicted, and also the soul be preserved."[16]

To William the Conqueror, who took offense over a bad joke told about him by the king of France, and in revenge ordered the destruction of an entire French town, the idea of capital punishment was utterly repugnant. He wrote: "Interdicimus etiam ne quis occidatur vel suspendatur pro aliqua culpa, sed enerventur oculi et abscindantur pedes, vel testiculi, vel manus, ita quod truncus remaneat vivus." ("We forbid moreover that anyone be hanged or otherwise put to death, for any

[14] J. Talboys-Wheeler, *History of India,* vol. 1, p. 74.
[15] Sir James Stephen, *History of the Criminal Law of England,* Macmillan & Co., London, 1883, vol. 1, p. 458 *et seq.*
[16] Thorpe, *Ancient Institutions of England,* Public Record Office, London, 1840, 1, 494.

offense whatsoever. But in such instances, his eyes may be put out, his feet cut off, or his testicles, or his hands; and in such manner only as to allow the rest of his body to go on living.")

This readiness, under any circumstances, to preserve some spark of life in a convicted malefactor was, of course, none too rigidly adhered to, and was soon enough abandoned. By the time of King Henry III (1216–1272), the sentence of death had become standard procedure in dealing with persons whom the state did not care for, even though the practice of now and again chopping off a lip, or nose, or hand was far from discontinued. For offenses termed "misdemeanors" as distinguished from "felonies" the penalty of mutilation continued to be favored by the authorities. At the time of the Commonwealth, Parliament decreed that in convictions for murder, "It shall be part of the judgment pronounced upon against every such offender that their right hand shall be cut off before their life be taken away."[17] For duelling, a form of warfare which the Puritans disliked intensely, the penalty was likewise the loss of the right hand, a punishment common to this very day in Muslim countries for stealing.

In England, as elsewhere throughout Europe, the death penalty in the course of medieval times came to be inflicted indiscriminately for the killing of a man and the killing of the king's deer, for sleeping with a nun or sleeping with the king's daughter-in-law, for stealing a shilling, or falsifying a will. During the reign of Henry III in the thirteenth century, eleven felonies, or capital crimes, were recognized in all. About one hundred years later, Bracton, in his systematic treatise of the laws, was able to list as many as thirty felonies.[18] "Progress" did not stop there. Under the Common Law, that is to say, the body of collected judicial decisions which the English were the first to compile and to treat as binding precedents, the number of such felonies continued to grow apace. Additionally, the "Mother of Parliaments" from the time of its inception in the late thirteenth century was absorbed in the enactment of laws calling

[17]Stephen, *op. cit.*, vol. 2, p. 209.
[18]*Ibid.*, p. 206.

for additional death sentence, over and above those decreed under Common Law. In all, Parliament, in the course of several centuries, was credited with creating its own catalogue of some one hundred and sixty capital crimes. Under the impact of developing commerce and growing economic complexity, the number of felonies continued to luxuriate, and always with the same incommensurable penalties. The incidence of the death penalty was thus molded with the times, and oddly enough seemed to follow the advancement of the times.

That which provided the sharpest edge to the movements in antiquity and later for introducing and extending the application of the death penalty was the need felt by rulers and governments to safeguard themselves against usurpers. Unlike murder, theft, or any of the common transgressions, there was never any question of a traitor or spy buying himself off by the payment of money. Treason was the original capital sin, more so than murder. Delicts against authority were, since remote times, taken far more seriously than those against humanity.

The sin of treason or resistance to authority has throughout the ages brought about the destruction of innumerable persons, depending often on the temper of the ruler and the interpretation that he chose to give to the alleged trespass. Almost anything could be viewed as being offensive or threatening, from circulating a scurrilous poem to sleeping with the king's mistress, or insulting his statue, or not approving of a royal marriage, or "imagining the king's death." At the time of the Tudor kings, Parliament enacted almost no legislation other than that of dreaming up new situations in which treason could be supposed.

There was rarely an escape from such an accusation, inasmuch as the function of judge and prosecutor invariably coalesced in the same person. Far more frequently than in prosecution for ordinary crimes, perjured testimony was a common ingredient in a great many of these "state trials." Perhaps the earliest reported instance of a trumped-up accusation of this character is that recorded in the Biblical book of I Kings. A proprietor by the name of Naboth had refused to sell his holding to King Ahab of Israel. On the testimony of two lying witnesses, he was then found guilty of having uttered remarks disloyal to the king, and was promptly stoned to death (I Kings 21).

In all countries, from Japan to the British Isles, almost any person of wealth unfortunate enough to attract the attention of his sovereign was at one period or another in some danger of being arraigned on political grounds. Accusations of this nature were also, from the standpoint of the royal exchequer, highly profitable in that condemnation invariably carried with it confiscation of the convicted man's property. The laws of treason, by providing a convenient means of striking at the rich, were thus a great equalizer between rich and poor.

Since treason was considered by far the most heinous of crimes, the simpler modes of inflicting death were not deemed sufficient punishment. In England, and in Europe generally, it was preceded and accompanied by ingenious methods of torture, such as drawing and quartering, crucifixion, breaking on the wheel, tearing with red-hot pincers, and boiling in oil. Once it became accepted that the normal and ordinary punishment for all crimes was death, steps were also taken to make it relatively more painful in some instances than in others. The outlandish and ghoulish sentences frequently meted out, by the supposed guardians of law and order, often made it difficult to determine whether the real criminals were the persons executed or those who sat in judgment upon them.

The German historian Menzel thus describes the man-devouring courts of his country during the age of the Reformation:

> The barbarous and dishonouring punishments inflicted by the degenerate Romans on their slaves were still enforced on the freeborn Germans. . . . Every township and provincial court had its torture chamber and place of execution. Wherever a hill commanding a lovely prospect rose in the vicinity of a town, its summit was crowned with a gallows and a wheel and covered with the bones of victims. The simple punishment of death no longer satisfied the pampered appetite of the criminal judge.

> Torture was formed into a system and horrors practised by the ancient tyrants of Persia and Rome, by the American savage in his warlike fanaticism, were, in cold blood, legalized by the lawyers throughout Germany.[19]

The "liberation of the human spirit" consequent to such great events as the invention of printing, the Renaissance, the discovery of America, and the Protestant Reformation seems to have exerted no moderating effect upon the fierce penal laws of that age. If anything, their administration became more sadistic and terrible. The most renowned jurists of the second and third centuries, such as Ulpian, Papinian, Paul, Gaius, and Modestinus, had acquiesced in the torturing of witnesses and of accused persons for the purpose of extracting confessions, along with crucifixion and other horrendous forms of judicial death-dealing. Many centuries thereafter, Benedict Carpzov, a jurist no less respected by his contemporaries, was credited with handing down at least 20,000 capital sentences while sitting in judgment at Leipzig between the years 1620 and 1660.

Now in the period of these intervening centuries the scope and influence of written laws had widened enormously. Centers such as Bologna, Paris, Oxford, Cairo, Beirut, Baghdad, and Samarkand had become the nurseries for legal studies. In both Christian and Muslim countries, some radical departures had by that time been made from the superstitious procedures of earlier times. Equitable rules governing civil status, commerce, and the transmission of property had been adopted. All such impressive rationalization notwithstanding, the original cruelty and barbarity of the penal laws remained untouched, and were in fact accentuated.

According to a study made recently by the Dutch historian, Johan Huizinga, the period of the late Middle Ages witnessed the upsurge of both legal and judicial ferocity to unheard-of levels.[20] Men chosen to sit in judgment on their fellows consid-

[19]Menzel, *op. cit.*, vol. 3, p. 1091.
[20]Johan Huizinga, *Déclin du Moyen Age*, Haarlem, 1947.

ered themselves entitled to exercise their utmost ingenuity in devising new and more terrible methods of inflicting death.[21] It was their fashion to consider the suspected criminals standing before them not as human beings, but as almost inanimate objects for whom all show of pity was irrelevant. Circumstances under which the offense had been committed, such as lack of intent, or obvious insanity, were brushed aside as being of no account.[22]

As pointed out by Huizinga, the fifteenth century, though in some respects a century of dawning enlightenment, was likewise a time of enhanced religious ferment and excitement. Torments, which are nowadays recoiled from in horror, were in the age of the Flagellants and Inquisitors looked upon as purgatives of the soul. Self-inflicted torments being viewed as acts of expiation, the dealing out of ordeals of a similar character to others was held to be salutary, since these too could be conducive to salvation in the world to come.

One person in keeping with the times was the German Dominican Jacob Sprenger, who devoted his entire life to hounding and destroying many hundreds of his countrywomen on the charge of witchcraft. After efficiently detecting and dealing with this particular transgression, he wrote a manual entitled *Malleus Maleficarum* (Hammer of Evildoers). It was first printed in Cologne in 1489. Between that date and 1669, this lamentable piece of literature was printed in twenty-six editions. Among the numerous specialists who found it a useful guide was a Bishop of Würzburg, who between 1625 and 1628 caused some 9,000 women of his diocese to be burnt alive, while in 1640 in the Silesian principality of Neisse there were

[21]In France until the beginning of the eighteenth century, all judicial officers purchased their posts from the king, with a chief justice paying upwards of 500,000 livres. It was not a system that offered much assurance of disinterest in matters of civil law, nor of decency in criminal cases (John H. Wigmore, *Panorama of the World's Legal Systems,* West Publishing Co., St. Paul, Minn., 1928, vol. 1, p. 265).

[22]In a review of Professor Huizinga's book, issue is taken with his thesis that all judges in France and the Low Countries were inhuman. A considerable list of exceptions is cited by L. T. Maes, "L'Humanité de la Magistrature du Déclin du Moyen Age," *Revue d'Histoire de Droit,* vol. 19, p. 158.

1,000 such victims.[23] These were only the more savage of many similar judicially ordered decimations.

In Britain of that period there were fewer burnings; but hangings and decapitations were plentiful. The predilection of English justice for the death penalty reached a high plateau at the time of the Tudor dynasty, remaining at about the same level for some two centuries thereafter. Until the year 1826, death was the expected price for high treason, murder, petty treason, arson, piracy, burglary, highway robbery, rape, manslaughter, abduction, forgery, smuggling, horse stealing, all thefts above the value of a shilling, and a large assortment of other felonies. No reliable statistics are available, but it has been claimed that in the course of the thirty-year reign of the psychopathic Henry VIII, as many as 20,000 English men, women, and children were judicially executed. An estimate worked out for the year 1598 placed the number of executions throughout the country at 800. For a population short of four million, this was a goodly percentage, and denoted a fair measure of insecurity on the part of the average Englishman.

Almost everywhere were present the showpieces of death to be gazed upon by both young and old. Shakespeare, on his way to the theatre, was grinned at by some thirty skulls mounted upon stakes between the fine houses of wealthy London burgesses on either side of London Bridge. Fifteen other theatres in various parts of London competed with his Globe Theatre. Other competition came from such entrancing public spectacles as the whipping of prostitutes at Bridewell, to say nothing of the hanging and disembowelling of both men and women at Tyburn—between twenty and thirty each day when the courts were in session.

The accelerated ferocity of the judicial process in an age of incipient enlightenment invites speculation as to the underlying cause. An upsurge in thievery was in fact favored by the revolutionary social and economic changes of the period in

[23]J. F. C. Fuller, *Decisive Battles of the Western World*, Eyre and Spottiswoode, London, 1963, vol. 2, p. 74n.

question. Then, as now, what was known as an "affluent society" implied both poverty and wealth existing alongside each other. Poverty had to be sufficiently intensified to induce more desperate men to embark upon a life of crime. Likewise, there had to be a sufficient increase in the number of newly rich for thieves to prey upon. Both these conditions were fulfilled in the period under review.

In Britain, the closing of about one thousand monasteries and nunneries by King Henry VIII resulted immediately in a vast number of already indigent persons being deprived of their one means of charitable assistance. This closing of religious houses was in effect a social revolution, which was soon copied in other countries as well. Compounding such misery of the common people was the drastic rise in the level of prices. Huge quantities of silver bullion from the mines of Mexico and Peru caused a catastrophic inflation, not only in Spain but in all of Western Europe. The working people whose wages were almost invariably frozen by custom were the main sufferers.

There were, however, many who benefited as a result of these upheavals and changes. The spoliation of the religious orders created a new set of rich property holders. The stimulation of commerce and industry consequent upon the discovery of the New World fostered a new class of merchants and producers. But even without the impetus of these overseas discoveries, the wealth of nearly all European towns and cities had been growing steadily from one century to another throughout that period known as the Middle Ages. The enlargement of the urban economy meant more travel along roads and highways. Such traffic, in its turn, could not but present many temptations to some of the more active spirits among the rural population.

Suggestive of the intertwined relationship between economic development, enhanced thievery, and sterner measures of suppression, a distinguished historian has written: "Highway robbery was from the earliest times a sort of national crime. . . . We know how long the outlaws of Sherwood lived in tradition. . . . These, indeed, were the heroes of vulgar applause; but when such a judge as Sir John Fortescue could exult that more Englishmen were hanged for robbery in a year than French in seven, and that if an Englishman is poor, and sees another having riches, which may be taken away from him by might, he will not spare to do so, it may be perceived how thoroughly these sentiments had pervaded the public mind."[24]

Now the boastful Sir John perhaps unduly disparaged the zeal of French judges by comparison with those of his own country. On the testimony of a thirteenth-century French chronicler it would certainly seem so. We are informed, "All over France you will find a gallows almost as common a sight in the landscape as a castle, an abbey, or a village. Many a fine spreading tree by the roadside has a skeleton dangling from one of the limbs. It is a lucky family of peasants which has not had some member thereof hanged, and even then plenty of rogues will die in their beds. Considering the general wickedness abroad, it seems as if there were a perpetual race between the criminals and the hangman, with the criminals well to the fore."[25]

To rectify a possibly one-sided impression, the reader should be reminded that the cruder forms of thievery, for which hanging was the accepted cure, were not monopolized by that body termed "the masses." The larcenous activities of a major portion of the noblesse of Germany, France, England, and Scotland are too well documented to require much in the way of reference. The proletarian Robin Hood had his counterpart in the knightly Goetz von Berlichingen who enjoyed a fabulous reputation among his contemporaries. Like the ineffable Robin, he lived on in a hallowed tradition among his fellow countrymen to be immortalized in one of Goethe's most dramatic masterpieces.

The suggestion has been made that if it were possible for us to recover the local annals of the various countries, they would reveal to us a mountainous accumulation of petty rapine and tumult.[26] The unbridled sadism of the penal laws was undoubt-

[24]Hallam, *History of the Middle Ages*, J. Murray, London, 1846, p. 247.
[25]William S. Davis, *Life on a Mediaeval Barony*, Harper, New York, 1923, chap. 10.
[26]Hallam, *op. cit.*, p. 247.

edly a reflection of the unruliness of the population, both high and low, compounded by excessive social inequality, administrative confusion, incessant warfare, and all-round brutality. Niccolo Machiavelli in his *History* refers to a horrendous event of the year 1343 when the dictatorial Duke of Athens was compelled by an angry mob to flee the city, while his less fortunate allies were seized in the streets, torn to pieces, their limbs paraded on sticks, and in some instances eaten by the triumphant activists.[27]

As the foregoing passage would indicate, a vicious circle of accumulated popular resentment and governmental retaliation was often the pattern. In a great many other instances, on the contrary, the prevailing picture was that of a common bond of wickedness and savagery between rulers and ruled, between exploiters and exploited. The general violence of private manners and popular passions, embracing both rich and poor, did not exclude an attitude of laissez faire towards the harsh penal laws. Accepted by all as part of the nature of things, there was a willingness, and even pleasure, on the part of a large enough segment of the population to witness and enjoy the last torments of the condemned. This popular trait, which seems to have remained unreformed down to the nineteenth century in the more civilized portions of the globe, remains unchanged in certain countries to this very day.

In England as late as the eighteenth century, the hanging of thieves in public invariably took on a festive character; and as a medium for amusing the public, it rivalled bear-baiting and theatre-going. In London, at the famous Tyburn tree (close to where now stands Marble Arch) an immense throng of sightseers would wait around impatiently for the gruesome exercises to begin. Peddlers and strolling jugglers entertained them the while. The condemned were driven to the place of execution from Newgate prison, the present site of the Old Bailey, in open carts called tumbrils. The route would be lined with crowds, some among them jeering, others cheering, or offering

[27]Niccolo Machiavelli, *History of Florence and the Affairs of Italy*, Walter Dunn, London, 1901, p. 100.

words of encouragement and refreshments in such instances where a particular candidate happened to be a popular figure or an admired highwayman whose luck had run out. At the journey's end, the enrapturement of the audience was unbounded, since death by hanging was then a slow process.

Voices of protest at the prevailing callousness began to be raised, however. To the eighteenth-century novelist, Samuel Richardson, it seemed a wonder to behold "men, women, and children in a kind of mirth as if the spectacle they beheld had afforded pleasure instead of pain." Even in the early part of the seventeenth century, Lord Chief Justice Coke did lament the spectacle "of so many Christian men and women strangled on that cursed tree of the gallows." (Without doing anything about it, however.)

THE GRADUAL ABROGATION OF THE DEATH PENALTY

In the first part of the present chapter the accent was placed on the widening application of the death penalty, historically speaking. In this part stress will be laid on its gradual abrogation, bearing in mind always that in the progression of neither of these opposite tendencies is any methodical chronology to be observed.

Our own time, no less so than that of the past, speaks not with one voice but with many. The movement of exalted humanitarianism, which has achieved its climax in the total abolition of the death penalty, seems anachronistic in a world beset by a renewal of large-scale barbarism and callousness.

In Soviet Russia and Red China, penal administration, far from having been influenced by any current of humanitarianism is, if anything, a reversion to the virulence of infant societies. The measure of crime is not the injury done to society, but to the regime in power. Where fanaticism and suspicion are clothed with the trappings of power, assaults upon all suspected nonconformists are commonplace. The category of political crime becomes uppermost, and overshadows all common offenses in point of seriousness. To implant fear and dejection in the breasts of all possible critics and opponents of the regime is the overriding concern.

In the U.S.S.R., the death penalty was abolished, officially that is, by Stalin in 1947, but not for long.[28] It was restored some three years later, by the same dictator, for an impressive list of improprieties, including treason, espionage, wrecking government property, terrorist acts, and banditry. By way of afterthought, the death penalty was restored for murder in 1954, murder apparently not being the greatest of all crimes on the Soviet calendar. In a land where no great emphasis is placed on the sanctity of human life, its violation does not constitute an offense of the first magnitude.

In 1961 and again in 1962, years after Stalin's passing, the Soviet death penalty was further extended to take in theft, counterfeiting, speculating in foreign currency, the taking of bribes, and rape.[29] The list of iniquities detailed in the Soviet criminal code is of course far from being inclusive. There are other sins against Soviet authority, not formally mentioned, that could place an offender in deadly peril. Major General J. F. C. Fuller, writing of the Hitler invasion of Russia, mentions the lack of documentation on the Russian side, and concludes that since in Russia the writing of history is subordinated to politics, no general would dare write his memoirs. Colonel G. A. Tokaev, a Caucasian officer in the Russian army who in 1948 sought refuge in the West, wrote: "It must be remembered that in the Soviet Union an attempt to reconstitute the true history of even the recent past is considered a capital offence."[30]

To a very large extent likewise, a sentence of imprisonment is equivalent to a sentence of death. Comparatively, few emerge from any stay in a Soviet prison camp with their health unimpaired. There is reason enough to believe that two centu-

[28]Berman, *Justice in the U.S.S.R.*, p. 86.
[29]According to John Gunther, Moscow has comparatively little crime. "Security is for the normal person complete; anyone can wander around anywhere at night in perfect safety" ("Moscow Revisited," *Reader's Digest*, January 1969).
[30]Colonel G. A. Tokaev, *Betrayal of an Ideal*, as quoted in Fuller, *Decisive Battles*, vol. 3, p. 425.

ries after the time of Beccaria, the torture of witnesses was and is still prevalent inside the vast Soviet dungeon. The alleged confession of a certain Savinkoff at his trial in Moscow in 1924 to the effect that he had been paid $200,000 to assassinate Lenin by the venerable and revered president of Czechoslovakia, Dr. Thomas Masaryk, was in all probability obtained by means of judicial torture.[31]

The attitude towards crime and criminals within the contemporary world is thus one of extremes. Quite obviously in the case of Soviet Russia, the reversion to a regime of judicial terror characteristic of mankind's darkest ages is a mirror of its internal social, economic, and political situation. The present government of Russia, built as it is upon an untenable and unworkable economic system, can maintain itself only by means of cruelty and fear. Feeling itself under constant threat, it is driven to maintain itself by means of a threatening posture of its own. Coincident with the extreme severity and harshness prevalent in the lands of the Iron Curtain is the opposite extreme of indulgence, which has become the rule everywhere within the free world. Nowhere is this attitude of permissiveness and tolerance more visible than on the North American continent.

No less striking is the contrast between Christian and Muslim countries in their respective attitudes towards erring citizens. The Islamic approach towards all sinners was summed up in the Koran in the famous Sura of the Prepared Table, which is found in the thirty-seventh verse of the fifth chapter, and which reads as follows: "The reward of those who make war against God and his apostle, and strive after violence on the earth, is that they shall be slaughtered or crucified or their hands cut off and their feet on alternate sides." Throughout the Islamic world of today, there is little evidence of any great change in this hard line.[32]

I shall now examine the several stages by which the law's

[31] *Time,* May 24, 1968.

[32] For an adequate portrayal of the manner in which the penal laws of the Koran were put into practice a few decades ago, see Wigmore, *Panorama,* vol. 2, pp. 614–637.

most dreaded edicts were gradually abridged throughout the Christian world, and finally eliminated in their entirety. The humanization of the criminal law has been one of the great achievements of the past two centuries, a period that has been rich in many-sided reforms. Nonetheless, the agitation against the death penalty reaches back to an even more remote period in European history.

The successfully invoked principle of Benefit of Clergy, a cause for which Thomas à Becket suffered martyrdom, was in effect an incipient revolt against the extreme severity of the secular laws, as well as the profuse application of the death penalty. To be sure, this agitation was only manifested on behalf of a restricted category of the population. Since a very early period in the history of England, and indeed of Christendom generally, all persons connected with Holy Orders were subject to the Canon Law of the Church and to its ecclesiastical tribunals. These persons, sheltered by their religious status, were exempt from the stern penalties prescribed by the secular penal laws. At these ecclesiastical courts, the punishment laid down for the most serious transgressions was the performance of acts of penance, such as the undertaking of pilgrimages to certain shrines. The extreme punishment was imprisonment for life in the Bishop's prison.

Now at the very beginning, Benefit of Clergy was reserved only to those who possessed "habitum et tonsuram clericalem," that is to say, to those who were actually tonsured and clothed as belonging to Holy Orders. As time went on, however, this benefit became available to a more extended category, including persons able to read and write, those who knew Latin, and undergraduate students of the universities. In the year 1350, Parliament, going even further, decreed that "all manner of clerks, as well secular and religious, shall henceforth enjoy the privileges of Holy Church as well as to persons not strictly in orders but assistants to them in doing Divine service, such as doorkeepers, readers, exorcists, and sub-deacons." That the year 1350 should mark this curtailment of the customary and legal death penalty in favor of a broad new category of England's inhabitants is highly suggestive. By the year 1350, the devastating Black Death had been raging for some three years, and had by that time carried off a large proportion of the population. The need to preserve the living assumed a hitherto unknown urgency.

The emergency of a drastically diminishing population having passed, we are informed that "the result was to bring about for a great length of time a state of things which must have reduced the administration of justice to a farce. Till 1487, anyone who knew how to read and write might commit murder as often as he pleased, with no other result than that of being delivered to the ordinary to make his purgation. . . . That this should have been the law for several centuries seems hardly credible, but there is no doubt that it was."[33]

Resulting from accident, or perhaps willful oversight on the part of some authorities, such inviolability was not a sure thing. According to one reliable report dating from the year 1402, a couple of thieving undergraduates from the University of Paris were unceremoniously hung and gibbeted on orders of the Provost of that city. In the eyes of all, this was obviously a disregard of the immunity due to youths of higher learning. The indignant faculty of the University immediately complained to the king of this high-handed official. It resulted in this ignorant fellow's being deprived of his office, ordered to return for dignified burial the bodies of the slain intellectuals, and ordered to erect at his expense a stone cross to the memory of their agony.[34]

Benefit of Clergy, found to be a serious barrier in the war against crime, and obviously a violation of the basic principle that all are equal before the law, was gradually done away with by a chain of parliamentary enactments, extending to the early part of the nineteenth century. In 1547 (*1 Edward VI*, c. 1) Benefit of Clergy was withdrawn in all cases of murder, highway robbery, housebreaking, stealing from churches, and arson. But for a long time thereafter it still remained a means of

[33]Stephen, *op. cit.*, vol. 1, p. 483.
[34]Robert Louis Stevenson, *François Villon.*

evasion for a host of other offenses normally punishable by death. Also, whenever a wanted criminal, regardless of his status, succeeded in reaching the shelter of a church, he won for himself the right of sanctuary, that is to say, he would no longer suffer condemnation of death. He would be permitted, after making the required confession, to leave the country unharmed, on vowing never to return. The absurdity of this unwarrantable extension of the rule enunciated in Deuteronomy 19:2–6, was later realized. This privilege of sanctuary was withdrawn early in the seventeenth century.[35]

Benefit of Clergy, though certainly one-sided and discriminatory, was in a sense a measure of protest against the unalloyed sadism of the penal laws. At the same time, the suppression of such blatant favoritism tended to bring in a degree of rationalization, along with a glimmer of humanitarianism whose benefit was available to all. By act of Parliament of 1677, "all punishments pursuant of ecclesiastical censures" were abandoned. From then on burning alive for heresy and witchcraft ceased.[36] The last reported instance of burning alive for the crime of heresy was in the year 1612, when by order of King James I, Bartholomew Legate was burnt at Smithfield for having denied the divinity of Christ. In 1666, the philosopher Thomas Hobbes of Malmesbury was for some time in danger of undergoing a similar fate.[37]

Yet another milestone was the famous Bill of Rights of 1689, under which "cruel and unusual punishments" were formally outlawed.[38] Prior to that time, the infliction of death took on a variety of ghastly forms, often meticulously enunciated in the law texts, or else left to the inventive imagination of the presiding justice. Burning alive for such offenses as poisoning or for sheltering rebel fugitives was prescribed by parliamentary statutes. During the short reign of the detested James II, late in the seventeenth century, no less than 233 persons were said to have been hanged, drawn, and quartered in the county of

[35]1 *James I*, c. 25; see also *20 James I*, c. 19.
[36](1) *29 Charles II*, c. 9.
[37]Stephen, *op. cit.*, vol. 2, p. 467.
[38]1 *William & Mary*, sess. 2, c. 2.

Somerset alone, in the course of a visit of only a few days of the notorious Judge Jeffreys. Some years later his granddaughter, the countess of Pomfret, while on an innocent journey through this same territory, was barely rescued from the vengeance of a mob, when her identity was accidentally discovered.[39]

The provision of the Bill of Rights notwithstanding, burning alive occasionally occurred during the enlightened eighteenth century. A seventeen-year-old servant girl, Margaret Troke, would have remained entirely unremembered by posterity had her punishment for robbing and then poisoning her mistress been merely another hanging. She was burnt to death at Winchester in 1738.[40] Only in 1790 was burning alive specifically outlawed by act of Parliament after a full century during which there had been some doubt whether it constituted a "cruel and unusual punishment." Throughout Western Europe, at about that time, the more atrocious forms of judicial death-dealing were removed. It is worth commenting upon that during the carnage of the French Revolution, when some ten thousand or more persons were guillotined for not believing in Liberty, Equality, and Fraternity, actual torture was not a conspicuous feature.

The humanization of the penal laws is to be seen not only under the aspect of the softening of the penalties, but not less so in the reform and rationalization of trial procedure. The iniquity and cruelty of the penal laws lay not only in the fact that these were excessively severe but also in the number of blameless lives devoured by them from day to day. Not so many centuries ago, a public execution was not any less frequent a mode for departing this life than cancer or heart disease in our own time. Even with a conscience that was in perfect order, one had to be exceedingly careful, among other things, as to the choice of his enemies. "A person with a bad name is already half-hanged," was the current proverb. For any peasant to make himself unpopular with his neighbors was often as good as committing suicide.

[39]Granger, *Biographical History,* Jeffreys.
[40]J. H. Plumb, *The First Four Georges,* Collins, p. 17.

In lifting the curtain from some of the monstrosities of ancient justice, note should here be taken of the irrational and superstitious practice known as trial by ordeal. Invariably, the administration of the ordeal was to doom both the guilty and the innocent, not only to death, but to some preliminary agony as well. It was a system that dispensed with witnesses, but relied on divination and the supposed intervention of the Almighty. Fairly widespread at one time over all the continents, it persists to this very day inside tribal Africa. In the Congo, prior to the coming of the Belgian "imperialists," an ordeal administered by tribal authorities to accused persons, by forcing them to take poison, claimed as many as fifty thousand lives in the course of a single year.[41]

The antiquity of this form of grotesque justice is attested to in ancient Greek literature; there is a passing reference to it in the play *Antigone* by Sophocles. The ancient Hindu code of Manu proclaims, "He whom the blazing fire burns not, whom the water forces not to come up quickly, who meets with no speedy misfortune must be held innocent."[42] Not only were you presumed at the very outset to be guilty, but it required nothing less than a miracle to prove you innocent.

Even in the Mosaic code we come across a survival of this thaumaturgy. In the case of an errant wife suspected of infidelity to her husband, she could be called upon to prove her innocence by drinking "the bitter water that causeth the curse," that is, a mixture of holy water and dust from the tabernacle. If this concoction caused "her thighs to rot" and "her belly to swell," her guilt was proven (Numbers 5:15–28). Much would depend on the woman's digestive powers, as well as the amount of solid matter that the officiating priest chose to include in the potion.

In the English practice, a hot iron weighing from one to three pounds had to be carried a measured distance, or else the suspect was invited to plunge his hand up to the wrist or elbow into a tub of boiling water for some number of minutes as the

[41]Jean Pierre Hallet, *Congo Kitabu*, Fawcett Publications, p. 66.
[42]F. Max Muller, *Sacred Books of the East*, vol. 25, p. 274.

presiding official might determine. The hand in question was then sealed up and kept bound for three days. If after being unbound the member showed any raw flesh, its owner was deemed guilty. Should there have been no such condition—a far less probable outcome—he was judged innocent.

There was, to be sure, some degree of primitive logic in this disastrous method. Actual culprits convinced that detection was unavoidable would consider it best to confess their guilt in order not to be punished twice over. In the case of innocent persons, the result was of course deplorable. Finding themselves in a hopeless dilemma, they would seal their own doom, when strong in the knowledge of their own virtue, or else from despair, they would be misled into believing that the natural course of things would be reversed in their favor.

Even to an age profoundly steeped in superstition, the utter insanity and malevolence of the system of ordeals became apparent. The final and unequivocal interdiction of trial by ordeal was dictated at the Fourth Lateran Council of the Catholic Church in the year 1215, after which such trials became infrequent both in England and on the Continent.

But a century in which decapitation, burning, hanging, and torture in the name of justice remained unabated, witnessed the abolition of one form of barbaric practice only to be succeeded by another, almost identical in substance. "The Inquisition, first introduced in the south of France late in the thirteenth century, was so successful in uprooting and discovering heresy, and its methods were so wonderfully efficacious —at least from a prosecutor's point of view—that they were adopted by most European countries. Hence secret trials, failure to confront the accused with the witnesses against him, refusal to allow him the benefit of counsel, and above all torture to wring out confessions came into European criminal procedure and remained to plague it for centuries."[43]

The latter half of the eighteenth century witnessed a mounting outcry against the excessive infliction of the death penalty

[43]Joseph R. Stanger and Dana C. Munro, *The Middle Ages 395–1500*, Appleton-Century-Crofts, New York, 1959.

along with its associated evil, the torture of accused persons and witnesses. The Methodists, a new denomination organized in 1739 by the brothers John and Charles Wesley, were foremost among these humanitarians. These men were also concerned with such other social abuses as Negro slavery and the ill-treatment of factory workers.

Cesare Beccaria of Milan was preeminent among writers of the period whose memory is associated with sweeping away "the debris of barbarous times." He published in 1763 his celebrated treatise *Of Crimes and Punishments.* Up to that time, the criminal legislation of all European countries, with the exception of England, permitted and even enjoined the use of torture. Beccaria was probably the first effectively to anathematize this irrational and brutal practice. There is almost no doubt that his epochal treatise was spurred by an act of judicial murder perpetrated shortly before by the Parlement de Toulouse. In 1760, Jean Calas, a respected merchant of that city and a leading member of the Protestant community, was declared guilty of having murdered one of his sons, supposedly on the ground that the victim—who was actually a suicide—was on the point of converting to Roman Catholicism. In the course of the trial, which contemporary observers branded as farcical and devoid of all justice, the wife and surviving son of the accused merchant were "presented" to the instruments of torture. The condemned man was put to a protracted and excruciating death. Voltaire, Rousseau, the queen of England, and the empress of Russia were among the many to denounce this affair as a murderous fraud, with the result that King Louis XV felt obligated to make some financial restitution to the heirs of the condemned man.[44]

Seldom before, or since, did a plea for reform meet with so instantaneous a repentance as greeted that of Beccaria. Almost immediately, the Austrian empress, Maria Theresa, whose rule took in that of Milan, decreed the abolition of the torture of witnesses in all criminal trials throughout her dominions. Most

[44]For a detailed version of this melancholy affair and its repercussions throughout Europe, see Frank Milton, *More Than a Crime,* Pall Mall Press, London.

European governments soon did likewise. In one other respect, however, the great teacher and reformer failed to see the realization of his purpose. The entire world, without exception, remained deaf to his plea for the total abolition of the death penalty.

Beccaria, it should be noted, was a decent and compassionate man. He was well in advance of his time in that he was horrified by all manifestations of legalized barbarism still acquiesced in by nearly all his contemporaries as part of the natural order of things. For anything beyond the mere outlawing of judicial torture, the intellectual climate of the time was still unprepared. The penalty of death, on guilt being proven, continued as beforetime to be inflicted by the slow strangulation of those that were hanged, and with even greater suffering to those expedited out of the world by other devices. For the most part, the victims of sadistic justice were not hardened criminals but minor offenders driven by hopeless poverty. Penalties of death continued to be handed down by magistrates calloused by routine, not infrequently revelling in cruelty, and eager only to get back to their routine pleasures. Many of these representatives of the law were of less moral worth than those whose lives they wantonly ordered to be extinguished. For a humane and sympathetic onlooker it was natural enough to become outraged at the entire system, and to cry out against a penalty that was exacted all too frequently and indiscriminately.

A word of caution is here required. Beccaria's negative opinion on this matter actually contains little or no comfort for the fervent abolitionists of today who not infrequently appeal to his authority. Beccaria's argument in favor of life imprisonment for murder, as opposed to the death penalty, is illuminating and merits being quoted.

> It is not the terrible but transient spectacle of a criminal's execution, but the long sustained example of a man's loss of liberty, of a man paying for his offence against society by labours resembling those of a beast of burden, which is the most powerful

> brake upon crime. . . . Now there is no one who on reflection would choose the total permanent loss of his individual liberty no matter what advantages a crime might bring him. It follows that the severity of a sentence of imprisonment for life, substituted for the penalty of death, would be as likely to deflect the most determined spirit—indeed I should think it more likely to do so.
>
> A great many men contemplate death with a steady tranquil courage, some out of fanaticism, some out of vanity, which attends us again and again to the very edge of the grave, some out of a last desperate effort to free themselves from life and misery; but neither fanaticism nor vanity can subsist among fetters and chains, under the rod, or under the yoke, or in the iron cage, where desperate man begins rather than ends his misery.[45]

Now the prisons of which Beccaria wrote were without exception in an infamous condition, and Beccaria was no prison reformer. The kind of life imprisonment that he envisaged as an alternative to executions would nowadays be rejected as excessively unmerciful, not only by opponents of the death penalty but hardly less so by its supporters. In our new age, in which life imprisonment exists in theory only, and in which most prisons have become comfortable abodes equipped with salubrious accommodations, the kind of detention advocated by Beccaria as an alternative to the infliction of death seems entirely out of place. To this eighteenth-century reformer, whose writings betray not the slightest sympathy for murderers, the arguments currently depended on by opponents of the death penalty would have seemed utterly bizarre. A suggestion that the lives of such creatures as the brothers Kray must be preserved because they are too sacred to be taken away would have left him dumbfounded.[46]

The watering down of capital punishment was an unsteady and wavering process, in which complicated elements were mixed together. I have suggested that the notable increase in wealth and in urban development after about the middle of the thirteenth century gave rise concurrently to an expanded

[45]From Alessandro Manzoni, *The Column of Infamy*, Oxford University Press, London, 1964, pp. 46–47, 49. The full text of Beccaria is included in this book.

[46]For a detailed and lengthy report on the criminal careers of the Kray brothers, see *Montreal Star*, March 6, 1969; *Times* (London), March 6, 1969.

brotherhood of thieves, which in turn engendered fresh severities in the penal laws. However, another side effect of this economic revolution was the enlarged financial resources of the state. Enhanced wealth meant enhanced military power. As one century followed another, there came a growing demand for soldiers on a full-time and permanent basis.

For keeping the criminal element of the population at a manageable level, the crucible of war was a more and more appealing alternative to that of judicially ordained decimation. Queen Elizabeth I of England discovered that it was both economical and socially advantageous to fill the ranks of her militias with men otherwise destined for the gallows. But the method of fusing a host of domestic vagabonds and ne'er-do-wells into a disciplined army fit for engaging in foreign enterprises was probably developed by Gustavus Adolphus of Sweden during the German Thirty Years War.[47]

Coinciding with the birth of England's overseas empire, the practice of reprieving condemned criminals also became common, on condition that they be transported at first to the American colonies and later to Australia. The initial settlement of New South Wales in January 1788 included six convict transports carrying 736 prisoners whose original death sentence had been commuted.[48] During the eighteenth and early nineteenth centuries, pardons conditional upon transportation to the colonies were said to have been granted in the great majority of capital convictions.[49] Notwithstanding, the number of hangings carried out from week to week remained impressive.

In France, it would seem, there were at all times fewer capital offenses on the law books than in England. Under an ordinance of 1670 (in the reign of King Louis XIV), 115 such offenses were listed, as against over 300 in England.[50] This disparity is understandable when it is remembered that in

[47]S.P. Wise, and H.O. Werner, *Men in Arms*, Praeger, New York, 1962, p. 107.
[48]Morris and Howard, *Studies in Criminal Law*, Clarendon Press, Oxford, 1964, p. 16.
[49]Stephen, *op. cit.*, vol. 1, p. 487.
[50]Figures given in speech of Mr. Alcide Simard, M.P., before Canada's House of Commons, March 22, 1966.

France there was no Parliament absorbed in the task of creating new capital crimes; nor did the French system recognize as necessarily binding judicially created penalties as was the practice under the English Common Law. With the coming of the French Revolution, neither the Constituent Assembly nor the Convention was apparently in the mood to cut down on the number of capital crimes. However, under the new penal code of 1810, promulgated by Emperor Napoleon, there was a significant reduction to thirty-six, while the Revolution of 1848 brought a further reduction to sixteen.

In England, during the time from 1770 to 1825—a period that was fruitful in reforms—the number of statutory offenses providing for the death penalty was drastically cut down. By 1825, there were still about 200 left. In 1826, during the reign of George IV, and in face of royal opposition, a single act of Parliament swept away by far the greater number, leaving a mere handful. There was some reversal of this trend in the legislation of 1827, 1828, and 1830, under which there was a reaffirmation of the death penalty for murder, piracy, robbery, burglary, sacrilege, housebreaking, theft above the value of five pounds from homes, stealing of sheep, horses and cattle, arson, destroying ships, attempts at murder by poisoning, administering poison to procure abortions, sodomy, rape, sexual relations with girls under the age of ten, forgery, forging transfers of share certificates, and making false entries in books of account. But again, soon thereafter, this category was felt to be unnecessarily broad, and was gradually narrowed down during succeeding decades of the nineteenth century.

The more recent steps to abolish capital punishment even for murder is of course the continuation of a long historical process, and has an acquired momentum. The climactic abolition of the death penalty within a number of leading countries of the free world can be seen under varying aspects and motivations. First carried out in Holland in 1860, the example was emulated by all of the Scandinavian countries before the close of the nineteenth century. Presumably within these nations, long noted for the placidity of their inhabitants, popular aversion to killing and violence had become so widespread as to suggest the complete doing away with a penalty which by that time was rarely applied in any event. But the situation was not similar in the United Kingdom, France, Germany, the United States, and Canada. Within these countries, at the very time when propaganda in favor of abolition finally gained its objective, there was no indication of any diminution of crime generally, or of murder in particular.

In Canada, one year after a proposal to abolish the death penalty had been decisively rejected, Parliament was persuaded to reverse itself, on being assured that abolition would be given a trial of five years, and that it would not apply to the killing of policemen. Ironically, a class of public servants, pilloried almost from day to day as practitioners of "police brutality," was here placed in a preferred category. It has not yet been explained why the killing of a policeman is a more serious matter than the assassination of a cabinet minister.

In the United States, where criminal laws are under state jurisdiction, no more than thirteen state legislatures have as yet been persuaded formally to outlaw the death penalty. *De facto* abolition, however, has been achieved throughout the country. In 1961, forty-one persons were executed throughout the U.S.A., in 1967 only two, and in 1968 none. The issue is of course intertwined with the delicate racial situation on the one hand, and the sociological climate on the other. "The kind of people who go to the death chair, even in northern states, tend to be poor and friendless, if not black. I cannot recall when a rich man was executed in this country."[51] Verdicts of murder have become exceedingly rare, virtually all cases of homicide being designated by such euphemisms as "first degree manslaughter" or "felonious assault." In the comparatively rare instances where verdicts of murder are actually rendered, the power of state governors to commute sentences of death is unstintingly used. Or some flaws in the proceedings are uncovered in appeal. The matter has been summed up by the expert

[51]Mrs. Eleanor Norton, assistant legal director of American Civil Liberties Union, as reported in the *Montreal Star*, January 9, 1969.

on capital punishment of the American Civil Liberties Union, Mrs. Florence Robbin. "The courts and governors of states are willing to accept any subterfuge to take the onus off them. They are reluctant to accept change in the law, but once the law has been satisfied by imposition of the death penalty, the courts will accept any maneuver to prevent it from being carried out."[52]

[52]As quoted in "U.S. Moves towards Abolition of Capital Punishment without Reforming Law," *Montreal Star*, January 9, 1969, p. 9.

CHAPTER 3

The Soft Sword of Justice

SOME UNSPECIFIED REDEMPTION HAS APPARENTLY BEEN envisaged for mankind following the discontinuance of the death penalty. Supposedly, the purpose of all sound legislation is to advance the well-being of the general public, or at least some deserving segment thereof. When, therefore, it was made known that for shooting, or stabbing, or poisoning no one need any longer stand in dread of the executioner, who, might it be asked, were the intended beneficiaries? By what process of ratiocination might it be shown that for the average respectable citizen, life and property have in this way been rendered more secure? On the contrary, it can be demonstrated all too effectively that for the socially disaffected, there has since been opened a new era of insolence tending to make crime a permanent profession instead of a sporadic adventure.

ON DOING GOOD TO WRONGDOERS

Anticapitalpunishmentism, on the eve of its victory, still makes further inroads and demands. Its dynamism is far from spent; it has now become the catalyst of a fresh outlook in crime in its many variations. Following hard upon the rejection of the death penalty, other forms of penalization have in their turn come under attack and criticism. A crescendo of protest has been released against "correctional institutions which do not correct" and "reformatory institutions which do not reform."[1]

The rationale of this momentum is in a sense indefeasible. By common consent, murder is no more than the principle highlight within a broad spectrum of impermissible acts. Since everyone is intended to be recompensed in proportion to the gravity of his offense, the scaling down of the sanction for murder ought logically to be attended, or followed, by some correlative adjustment as regards other breaches of the criminal code, including manslaughter, second degree murder, acts of mayhem, rape, arson, and larceny of every description. So perfected has been the spirit of forgiveness that there has indeed been a diminution of all penalties across the board, if we are to judge only by the significant decline in the prison population in both the United States and Canada. The report in a recent issue of *National Prisoners Statistical Bulletin of the United States Bureau of Prisons*[2] which indicated that during the period from 1961 to 1966, the country's prison population diminished from one year to another by percentages ranging from two to over five, is interesting in this connection. For Canada, the trend has been similar.[3] Canada's prison population declined from 7,600 in 1965, to 6,800 in 1968.

Throughout this continent there have been easements in every category of crime, some to the point of nullification. Sentences imposed, while utterly destitute of uniformity, have nevertheless been notably reduced from those formerly regarded as the norm. Homosexuality and obscenity are to all intents and purposes no longer punishable. For larceny and other offenses generally, the sentences are invariably far below the maximum prescribed in the written codes. Even arson may entail no more than a small fine.[4] The diminished sensitivity to crime generally also manifests itself in a blasé and sophis-

[1]For example, see "Some Sociological Aspects of Criminal Law," *Michigan Law Review*, vol. 13, p. 584.

[2]No. 43, August 1968.

[3]*Correctional Process* (publication of the Canadian Welfare Council), vol. 10, no. 1 (November 1968).

[4]For having set fire to six buildings, a Montreal man was fined $100 and sentenced to a very brief term of imprisonment *(Montreal Star*, April 30, 1969, p. 6).

ticated attitude towards the security of one's own country, coupled with an easygoing tolerance of its enemies. Under recent decisions of the Supreme Court of the United States, a known Communist may not be dismissed from his job in a war industry. A university professor may not lose his employment for teaching and advocating the overthrow of the government by force.[5] In Canada, procedural decisions of the courts have made it highly impractical to prosecute a public servant for selling state secrets.

As for murder, its downgrading as an unforgivable offense has not been arrested by the discontinuance of the traditional penalty. The substituted penalty of life imprisonment has in turn been watered down, so that it is held to be no more than a fiction. Also, under an abridged definition, many murderous acts are no longer catalogued as such. What was formerly deemed to be attempted murder is more often than not put down as "assault." For such homicidal acts, as were traditionally distinguishable from murder, the sentence is in many instances no more drastic than for theft or holdup, notwithstanding that politicians are wont to cry out that under all and any circumstances life is more important than property.

Beccaria, often cited as the major prophet for the amelioration of the penal laws, recommended that a clear distinction be made between theft pure and simple, and theft accompanied by violence or threat of violence. For the former, he proposed imprisonment; for the latter, a combination of imprisonment and bodily punishment. The use of the lash in the case of violent attacks upon peaceful citizens is still a feature of the criminal code of Canada, and has never been formally abrogated. Taking advantage of the all but unlimited discretion with which they have been clothed, judges, as well as parole boards and politicians, have acquired the habit of no longer separating persons accused of theft into violent and nonviolent categories. Day-to-day newspaper reports of court proceedings confirm this growing disregard of any differential be-

[5]Supreme Court Reports, re Robel, Dec. 22, 1967, vol. 19, p. 508; Supreme Court Reports, re Keyishian, Jan. 23, 1967, vol. 17, p. 629.

tween the dangerous and the nondangerous.

In the course of a ceremony held in Montreal honoring an officer of the Quebec Provincial Police for the single-handed capture of three gunmen holding up a bank, it was announced that of the three miscreants, one had received sentence of one month imprisonment, another of six months, and the third of one year.[6] It would serve no useful purpose to encumber the text with a repetition of similar examples, which the reader of any newspaper in any city of this continent may discover for himself. It suffices to refer to an opinion voiced by Director Adrien Robert of the Quebec Provincial Police who has revealed how the light sentences commonly meted out by the courts for armed robbery have encouraged criminals to turn to crimes of violence, resulting in possible homicide, in preference to lighter crimes. The confirmed thief, he has pointed out, nowadays finds it far more to his advantage to thrust himself into banks and other places of business for obtaining cash, rather than in making off with merchandise. The disposal of stolen goods is both bothersome and risky. Plain cash, on the other hand, involves no marketing problem, while at the same time the penalty to be feared is scarcely any greater than for unarmed theft. Eloquent testimony to this process of equalization is the fact that since 1962, crimes of violence within the Province of Quebec have nearly doubled. The separation, urgently prescribed by prison reformers, of the redeemable transgressor from the confirmed hoodlum having in practice ceased to be complied with, they are both as a matter of course often relegated to the same prison quarters. The horrifying consequences of the physically frail detainee being housed alongside the hulking terrorist have several times of late come forcibly to light.[7] For better or for worse, the abandonment of the death penalty for murder has brought in its wake a new deal for all offenders both great and small.

[6] *Montreal Gazette,* April 23, 1968.
[7] See "Our Sick Jails," *Reader's Digest,* February 1967; "Catalogue of Savagery," *Time,* September 20, 1968.

CONSEQUENCES

The abandonment of the traditional abhorrence of crime and criminals has already had some grand repercussions. Delivered as we have been from these prejudices, we witness in all the cities of this continent the saturnalia of crime, and we behold its offspring, street rioting and campus disorders, outrunning one another in the exercise of the new freedom. The contrast is indeed glaring between the repudiation of the "police state" and the ever increasing boldness and insolence of society's baser elements. An editorial in the *Montreal Gazette* of April 23, 1968, not inaptly entitled "Heavy Crime and Light Punishment," poses a highly pertinent question: "Who benefits from short sentences imposed for serious crimes? Certainly not the public which is exposed to an increasing number of crimes. Certainly not the police who have to arrest the same criminals, often dangerous criminals, over and over again. Certainly not the criminals themselves who, finding that the way of the transgressor is easy, are not reformed but encouraged in their criminal careers."

It could of course be argued that the mere following of one phenomenon by another does not necessarily presuppose a causal connection. The Latin maxim *post hoc ergo propter hoc* (after this, therefore because of it), stated as an absolute, has been criticized, and not altogether unjustly. This being conceded, the quantitative results that have followed so soon after the triumphant crusade against the death penalty must be examined on a calculation of probability. From every side, the statistical evidence that keeps pouring in about the rise in homicides, along with acts of violence generally, is of such consistency as to negate the probability that they are coincidental, or due to errors in the compiling of the facts.

The Royal Commission on Capital Punishment, set up by the British government in 1953 to probe into the matter of how far the death penalty had any influence on the rate of homicide, felt itself unable to uncover statistical evidence pointing one way or the other. For a variety of reasons, it could discern no kinship between the statistics of one country and those of another. The alternate method, that of comparing the rate of homicide within the same country or state or province during the period when the penalty was in force, with a similar period subsequent to its abolition, was likewise found to be unreliable, due to the distortion of gradual phasing out. Such were the early barriers to statistical comparisons affecting Britain, Canada, and the United States.

With the passing of the years since the time of the inconclusive findings of the Royal Commission, the integration and comparison of contrasting figures have come to present less of a problem. It should indeed be conceded that the problem of accurate statistical comparison has by no means been shorn of all difficulty. In Britain since 1957, a distinction has entered between capital and noncapital murder. In Canada, this distinction was adopted in 1960. As regards the United States, there is of course no uniformity of definition. Nonetheless, considering that all such change has invariably been a downgrading, all given figures on murder are in a sense deflated, and hence even more ominous than they appear.

The method of statistical comparison becomes less open to doubt once it ceases to concern itself with only one particular offense. The more detailed and variegated the measuring rod, the more reliable it becomes. Murder, by whatever definition, is only one of several facets in the crime picture. It is in general intertwined with other offenses, those relating to property for the most part. Thus, you are not likely to be informed of any increase in homicides in the absence of a similar announcement as regards lesser forms of violence. Furthermore—and I stress this greatly—the time that has elapsed since the abolition of the death penalty, whether legal or *de facto,* in Britain, the U.S.A., and Canada, has now been long enough to permit a less controversial interpretation of the crime statistics of all three countries. The upward curve of these figures, including the latest available, has been so uniform and consistent as to make it increasingly difficult to deny that the figures are all related to a common event.

In all three countries, following the repeal of the death penalty, the aftermath has been identical. With ever increasing violence, the criminal elements in each of these countries have stepped up their offensive against society, with the possibility of a law-abiding citizen becoming a victim rising from year to year. Criminal action in one form or another strikes one out of five families in the United States in the course of a single year.[8]

According to figures released by the Federal Bureau of Investigation, violent crime, expanding prodigiously from one decade to another, accounted for 250 victims for each 100,000 of the population in the year 1967. This was 57 percent higher than in 1960, 88 percent higher than in 1950, and more than double that of 1940. From 1960 to 1968, the national rate of criminal homicide per 100,000 of the population increased by 36 percent, the rate of forcible rape by 65 percent, of aggravated assault by 67 percent, and of robbery by 119 percent.[9]

For Canada, since 1957 (the year in which capital punishment was abolished *de facto*) the climb in the murder rate has been impressive, and more especially so since 1967 when the repeal was formalized. In 1957, the number of reported murders for every 100,000 of th population above the age of seven was 129. By 1968, this number had risen to 314, by almost two and one-half times. In the same period, the number of homicidal deaths, not related as murders, rose from 198 per 100,000 to 328.[10] The Province of Quebec, noted for its benign judiciary, has led all the other provinces in its contribution to the upsurge in crime, with an overall increase from 1967 to 1968 of 17 percent. Murder during that one-year period went up by 47 percent, bank robbery by 57 percent, breaking and entering by 21 percent, and theft from motor vehicles by 21 per-

[8] *U.S. News & World Report,* February 5, 1968.
[9] Federal Bureau of Investigation, "Uniform Crime Reports." See also statement of Dr. Milton Eisenhower, chairman of the National Commission on Causes and Prevention of Violence, released on November 24, 1969, as reported in *U.S. News & World Report,* December 8, 1969.
[10] *Dominion Bureau of Statistics 1968,* catalogue no. 85, p. 209.

cent.[11] The Province of Ontario, the richest and most populous of Canada, is also an outstanding exemplar of progress in crime. For the year 1967, the Ontario Police Commission reported some major "advances," with crimes of violence well in the van. In regard to murder, there were 96 in 1967 as against 56 in 1966, a tidy increase of 71 percent, as though in celebration of the formal abolition of capital punishment. Robberies were up by 39 percent. Burglaries totalled 40,549, a rise of 15 percent. Rape, until a few years ago punishable by death, increased by 20 percent, for a total of 212. There were in the same bountiful year 22,458 instances of assault, a "gain" of 14 percent, along with the wounding of 369 for a lesser increase of 6 percent. Far more telling was the 24 percent increase in the number of persons accused of carrying offensive weapons. Thefts of over $50.00 soared to 29,298, increasing by 13 percent.

The figures for the United Kingdom are somewhat less sensational. Nonetheless, "crimes of violence are increasing at a disturbing rate. There were 2,300 offenses involving firearms in 1967, compared with 730 in 1964."[12] While the increase in the number of murders has not been too significant, the number of armed robberies has been soaring. In London, there were 2,000 such cases in 1967 as compared with 250 in 1950, an eightfold increase, with a twentyfold increase in the actual property stolen.[13] By North American standards, the number of policemen attacked and murdered is still on the low side. The rate of about two policemen murdered each year is only four times as high as during the fifty years preceding the removal of the death penalty. In Scotland, there were 356 attacks on police in the three years from 1966 to 1968, as compared with 196 in the previous three years.[14]

Liberal-minded persons, highly impatient about all this to-do over crime, and having their own interpretation of this phenomenon, do not take kindly to all these measurements.

[11] *Montreal Star,* January 15, 1969.
[12] James Steward in *Montreal Star,* March 6, 1969.
[13] W. F. Deeds, M. P., in *Daily Telegraph,* May 17, 1969.
[14] *Montreal Gazette* February 20, 1970.

They inform us that they are "remarkably elastic," that they have been compiled by police officials themselves, that they depend upon the quality of reporting by the various police departments, and upon the desire of police officials "to dramatize the problems they face," as well as upon a "new focus on crime which translates into higher crime rates illegal acts which went unrecorded before." [15]

Now, Mr. Abrams is wrong on several counts. His reference to the police dramatizing the problems they face is in effect an allegation of some kind of conspiracy to hoodwink the public that would have to be leveled simultaneously at every police force in the United States, Canada, and Britain. The detailed picture of crime during a given period is compiled every three months by the Federal Bureau of Investigation on the basis of information supplied by local and state police agencies. The figures supplied have never been questioned as to their veracity by the Department of Justice, which releases them periodically. Nor have they been questioned by numerous judges, states attorneys, and members of Congress, whose use of such figures has never been challenged. It is also nonsensical to assert that the figures on murders, assaults, and bank holdups have at any time been padded by deliberately bringing in "illegal acts never before deemed sufficiently important to be recorded."

It is indeed significant that, according to a survey made in the United States by the National Opinion Research Corporation, about half the crimes committed throughout the country are not even reported to the police. It is suspected, for example, that among the 20,000 unexplained deaths each year of children, a goodly percentage are actually murdered by their parents. Obviously the crime statistics put out by the police and the Federal Bureau of Investigation, far from being exaggerated, are actually an understatement of the true situation.

Again, we have the further liberal tenet that "a careful balance must always be struck between society's need to protect

[15]Morris B. Abrams (president of Brandeis University), "Law and Order Platform," *Newsday;* reprinted in the *Montreal Star*, October 21, 1968

life and property and the individual's right to human dignity, privacy, and personal freedom." I would suggest, with all respect, that there is and should be no such balance. Society's need to protect life and property ought to be considered absolute, and subject to neither compromise nor balance with anything. And if by "the individual" is meant the killer and burglar, I would suggest likewise that his right to human dignity, privacy, and personal freedom ought to be counted as nil.

Of no little significance is the discovery that in such rare instances where the liberal approach has been abandoned, a reverse trend in criminality has resulted. A federal commission looking into the causes and cures of violence has been given an example of what happens in a city when its officials take a "tough line." This city is Philadelphia, whose district attorney, Arlen Spector, had this to say: "In Philadelphia, we have urged tough sentences for tough criminals. . . .We have increased the conviction rate on crimes of violence. . .the major crime rate in Philadelphia has dropped while crime around the nation has soared."[16]

THE THEORY OF THE SICK SOCIETY

Liberal-minded clergymen, professors, and politicians have their own interpretation of the soaring crime wave and have their own recommendations for counteracting it. "It is not enough for us to say that we are going to have law and order," Senator Charles Percy of Illinois told his colleagues of the United States Senate, "we must rectify wrongs in this country." The theory of a society covered with sores is of course basic to the wishful pessimism of socialist ideology. "The hungry masses steal in order to survive." For this situation, the only remedy is said to be "a sound knowledge of Marxism-Leninism, especially modern Marxist philosophy."[17] Liberals will of course have no part of this asinine therapeusis. Yet according to their mystique, the counterattack on crime is warrantable

[16] *U.S. News & World Report,* November 11, 1968.
[17] W. Loose and G. Stiller, *Staatsrecht,* Berlin, 1967, as quoted in a review in *Excerpta Criminiologica,* October 1968, p. 341.

not otherwise than as part of a total war against the imperfections of the state.

Now, all these wrongs afflicting the nation taken over a wide enough canvass are perhaps almost as numerous as are the critics who draw them to our attention. The problem is first to single out for closer examination those among them who could have some possible bearing on the crime situation. By way of bringing the investigation into more immediate focus, it could be suggested that a survey of opinion first be made among one hundred prison inmates, requesting them to tabulate those particular evils of society that have impressed themselves upon their minds. These one hundred lists so prepared should then be summarized into one single list. A similar questionnaire should be submitted to one hundred citizens, chosen at random among those who have never been confined in any prison; and that in their case, as well, all individual answers be consolidated into one master list of grievances. Now it is my contention, were such a hypothetical inquiry instituted, that two results would emerge. First, the list of society's shortcomings would in both cases be quite extensive; and second, they would in their details approximately duplicate one another. It could be quite safely conjectured that neither list would fail to mention such salient national shortcomings as high cost of living, unemployment, discrimination, war, lack of educational opportunities, pollution of air and water.

In Canada, the United States, Britain, France, and elsewhere in the free world, there are millions of persons who are acutely concerned and dissatisfied about many of the aspects of their respective societies, yet do not on such grounds resort to any criminal acts whatsoever. A great number give expression to their discontents by joining the many political parties that are dedicated to the removal of some or all of these grievances. Even the relatively small number who join up with political sects reputed to be extremist and irresponsible remain personally uninvolved with criminal activities.

Of more than ninety-nine percent of the "masses" it can be asserted that they have not been changed into criminals by the mere fact that they have sensed within the society in which they are living a large array of shortcomings and maladjustments. But what of the others? What are the compulsions that cause a small segment of the population to take to a life of crime? The United States, in common with many other nations, is presently confronted with a number of arduous situations, some of them remediable and others possibly not. The pollution of Lake Erie, for example, is recognized as a serious national problem. For cities bordering on this waterway, such as Cleveland, Toledo, and Sandusky, the situation is beyond doubt especially distressing. Yet it would be utterly absurd to surmise that this overhanging depressant has been responsible for changing any of the inhabitants of these cities into rapists, or swindlers, or drug peddlers. No one in New York City has become a looter or an incendiary because of a reduction in the American gold reserve, alarming though this might be to many. In Detroit, no one has taken to stealing automobiles because the pivotal automotive industry of the United States has been made to face some acute competition from foreign imports. There is hardly any reason to suppose that the failure to end the armament race or the war in Viet Nam or the trouble in the Middle East or the imbalance of international payments has ever turned anyone into a pickpocket or a housebreaker, or a bank robber or a forger or a kidnapper. Failure to solve these and other problems, both political and economic, certainly threatens the safety, prosperity, and even the very lives of millions of human beings. But let it be conceded, nonetheless, that solving them will not turn very many dishonest men into honest men, or professional assassins into harmless citizens.

Without entering upon the forbidding task of defining the perfectly healthy society, it is sufficient to declare that it does not exist anywhere and never will. Of the considerable number of failures and shortcomings that could possibly be pinpointed as disfiguring North American society, by far the greater number can immediately be ruled out as having little or no relevance to the crime explosion. There remain to be considered, notwithstanding, some blemishes inseparable from the social order whose bearing on crime is certainly direct, even though, as will be contended, they fall short of shedding any light on the reasons for such crime having been accelerated.

SLUMS AND GHETTOES

The quasi-masochistic doctrine that society is itself to blame for the criminal onslaught is founded on the belief that nearly always are dangerous and persistent lawbreakers the alumni of rundown urban areas deliberately left in that condition by an unfeeling "establishment."[18] The area within a city commonly designated as a slum is not easily distinguishable from a neighborhood populated mainly by factory workers. There is to be found within both these areas a sufficient number of foodstores, drugstores, furniture stores, clothing stores, automobile repair shops, and liquor stores. They are not wanting in doctors and dentists. They are supplied along with other districts with water, sewage disposal, lighting, and other civilized amenities, with the probable exception of adequate policing.

The main physical feature that may be said to distinguish many working-class neighborhoods, including such as have greatly deteriorated, is the juxtaposition of the homes with factories, warehouses, and shops, all being mixed together indiscriminately. It is an obvious advantage for wage earners to live in close proximity to their places of employment; but the attractiveness of their homes is almost certain to suffer as a result. While a high enough percentage manages to retain some air of neatness, even in bad localities, many become squalid on the outside, at least. Much depends on the nature of the housekeeping. While slatternly housekeeping will almost inevitably bring out the worst in the residents and their families, it is a moot question whether it is the substandard human being that really is to blame for the deterioration of buildings or the reverse. The answer to this question is of considerable import before it is decided to commit many billions of taxpayers' money to tearing down and rebuilding entire neighborhoods.

[18]This establishment was formerly anathematized by such terms as "exploiters," "capitalists," "bourgeoisie," and "imperialists."

That among those who go home to bed amid sordid surroundings there is an inordinately large number of disorderly men and women requires hardly any demonstration. However, such repugnant characteristics as coarseness of speech, sexual promiscuity, uncleanliness, idleness, and venereal disease by no means constitute the core of the crime situation. The charitableness here to be expected does not have to be extended to the hardened killers, muggers, rapists, and hoodlums.

A precinct-by-precinct analysis of crime was reported to the New York City Police Department by the *New York Times.* It revealed that within the slums there existed a heavier concentration of crime against both persons and property than in other parts of the metropolis. This survey also confirmed that the poor who populate these neighborhoods were invariably the more likely targets of both violence and theft.[19] A Negro was pronounced to be four times more exposed to being robbed than a white man. It is not farfetched to assume that following an effective roundup and penalization of some exceedingly scabrous "underdogs," the intimidated people in slum areas would be the very first to heave a sigh of relief.

Not all criminals were born and raised amid sordid surroundings. Families in easy circumstances have been prolific enough in generating all manner of ne'er-do-wells. Dr. William Belson, director of the Survey Research Centre at the London School of Economics, has revealed that although theft tended to increase with each step downward in the social scale, there was a substantial amount of it among the sons of professional, semiprofessional, and managerial men.[20] Theft can have its root causes not only in an overpowering desire for other people's possessions and in an inbred aversion to honest labor, but also in alcoholism and in drug addiction. Not one of these considerations is exclusive to any particular social stratum. While murder likewise can have its genesis in the search for easy money, it is often enough politically motivated, brought on by family feuds, or by sexual embroilment. Obviously, here too, no part

[19] *Montreal Star,* December 5, 1968.
[20] *New York Times,* September 10, 1968.

is necessarily played by the maladjustments of society.

An extensive category of criminal offenses, offenses which by their very nature require both capital and know-how, is altogether foreign to slums and ghettoes. Activities such as forging, counterfeiting, receiving stolen goods, importing narcotics, promoting prostitution and gambling, defrauding creditors and investors, setting fires, and a host of others not unrelated to the world's commerce, industry and politics are monopolized by the well-to-do. It has well been said that "the affluent society is a society of opportunists, which includes the dishonest as well as the industrious among its beneficiaries."[21] What sociological pleas, may it be asked, are being offered for this particular breed of lawbreakers? Perhaps some excuse is discoverable in that couplet of the eighteenth-century poet, Oliver Goldsmith, who wrote prophetically, "Where wealth and freedom reign contentment fails, and honour sinks where commerce long prevails."

POVERTY

Abolish poverty, we are often told, and you will abolish crime. Prevailing indigence does indeed help in bringing about evil deeds, but so too does affluence. There would not be nearly so many cases of larceny were it not for the fact that many automobiles are standing about waiting to be driven away. Handsomely furnished homes are an invitation to unwanted guests. Business establishments offer a dazzling array of clothing, furs, and jewelry to the honest and dishonest alike. Factories, warehouses, and financial institutions have their doors wide open to all comers.

Aristotle declared that poverty is the parent of crime. But Lucan (A.D. 39–65) was of the opinion that poverty is the mother of manhood. Both these ancients were in some measure right. Poverty, or at least the fear thereof, causes a host of young men and women to train themselves to become physicians, lawyers, engineers, nurses, stenographers, mechanics,

[21] J.J. Tobias, "The Crime Industry," *British Journal of Criminology* (July 1968).

bus drivers, playwrights, poets, and creative writers.

It is also trite to observe that the very concept of poverty admits of great fluidity of definition. A level of existence which in Harlem is considered penurious would not be so regarded in most European capitals. According to the Office of Economic Opportunity, the poor in the United States make up no more than 15 percent of the population.[22] Poverty in the United States can be said to be psychological as well as physical. But when people are chronically hungry and undernourished, their poverty is of course physical. There are conflicting reports as to how many Americans actually suffer from malnutrition.[23]

In the United States, with its wide and generous range of social benefits, it is doubtful if there is anyone at present who fails to receive enough income to ward off hunger. Malnutrition will persist—and it could be fairly substantial—only among those who will not spend intelligently whatever money they do receive. Starvation was at one time a motivation for thievery on a large scale. It has long ceased to be so, on this continent at least. Foodstores and supermarkets are not especially exposed to being burglarized, except for the money that could be left overnight in their tills. When homes are broken into—some two and a half millions a year, by recent estimate—the contents of the refrigerators are about the last things that the intruders are curious about.

In connection with crime, one should speak not so much about poverty, a most elusive concept, as about inequality, a concept whose definition presents no difficulty at all. A great many persons who have enough to eat, sufficient clothes to ward off the cold, homes in which they do not freeze, opportunities for education and medical care, are nonetheless hostile and embittered because, for one reason or another, they are unable to perform well in the crucible of normal everyday living.

[22] *Time*, May 17, 1968.
[23] For two differing versions, see articles in *Time*, May 17, 1968, and *U.S. News & World Report*, May 27, 1968.

Our age has witnessed the birth, or rather rebirth, of new political sects whose tenet is that because everything in the world is wrong, the inclination towards crime is nothing more than a justifiable form of "protest." This emphasis on social problems as the "root cause" for murder, rape, and hoodlumism is actually an offspring of a marriage between inequality and politics. It bears some distant resemblance to the mood of ancient Rome during the declining years of the Republic.

The times then as now have been favorable to the emergence of men skilled in exploiting class and racial hatreds for the furtherance of demagogic ends, as well as in fomenting "dissent" even among the sons of prosperous families. In all major cities, there is to be found a well-fed proletariat, pampered by the state and yet filled with bitterness. This class is being ably manipulated not only by ambitious politicians but by well-meaning clerics and professors, sensitive to all social ills, but usually quite ignorant of their causes. Among this flotsam, there are numerous violently disposed persons, who when apprehended are aided before the courts not only by able counsel, but by the outcries of obstreperous sympathizers. Many are thus released from custody without even being placed on trial. Others are frequently saved from punishment on feeble pretexts of nonobservance of their so-called rights. At the same time, the coercive power of the police, appointed for the protection of the law-abiding and the peaceable, is everywhere being corroded by a systematic campaign of denigrating slogans, making it ever more difficult to bring the average troublemaker to heel.

It is difficult to contradict the opinion expressed by J. Edgar Hoover: "Social and economic causes aside, there are other important factors which have a strong bearing on the era of violence we live in . . . crime and violence are increasing primarily because there is a mass deterioration in the respect shown for the rule of law in our nation and for some who enforce it. In addition the deterrents to crime have been weakened. Those who choose to break the law or commit acts of violence know that the punishment no longer fits the crime."

To delve more deeply into the causes of crimes is not the task which I have set myself in the present chapter, or in any other of this book. There are doubtless many causes. The problem is not to immerse ourselves in such fundamentals, but to inquire merely why it is that crime has been intensifying. In countries where the level of popular education is far lower than it is on this continent, and where the amount of comfort and prospertiy is known to be appreciably less, the problem of mounting crime is also less.

In neither Canada nor the United States has the condition of the slums within recent years taken any turn for the worse. Illiteracy has not increased. Poverty has not become more widespread. The contrary has been the case. In both these countries strenuous endeavors have been made to outlaw racial discrimination, and not without success. In the United States, the number of Negro families earning more than $7,000 a year has more than doubled since 1960. Astronomical sums have been devoted to the improvement of primary and secondary schooling, as well as to the retraining of adult workers and special courses for underprivileged adults. Millions of homes have been built in the poorer sections of nearly all the cities. In 1959, about 39 million Americans, or 22 percent of the population, had incomes below the "poverty line," as defined by the federal government. By 1967, the number so disadvantaged had fallen to 26 millions, or 13 percent of the population. Over five hundred agencies of the federal government have been dispensing grants in the neighborhood of fifty billion dollars annually. Such generosity, while perhaps insufficient for the achievement of perfection, is scarcely an indication of a society that is "sick."

HEREDITY AND ENVIRONMENT

The thesis that criminals by and large are by nature inherently well meaning, but that they have become spiritually bruised by the accumulated evils of the world deserves to be greeted with more than a measure of skepticism. Are, then, criminals born?

To pose such a question is like asking whether there are born philanthropists, or born liberators, or born revolutionaries, or born reformers, or born captains of industry?

Obviously, no person is at birth predestined to a career, unless possibly in the case of the heir to royalty. There are from the very outset of a person's life numerous environmental factors that ultimately determine whether he becomes a professional man, or a laborer, or a scientist. Nonetheless, all such incidental factors that determine the course of one's life, no matter how numerous and weighty, do not rule out the presence of certain inborn propensities, or talents, or characteristics. Are there persons who are born with less than average intelligence? The answer is clearly in the affirmative. Are there persons born with an innate gentleness of spirit? Here too, the answer is clearly that there are such persons. Are there persons who start out with an innate disposition to violence and an overdeveloped egotism? How can this be denied? This can only be denied by those philosophers who are determined to see the world in the image of their own preconceived notions of perfection.

To assert dogmatically that no one is ever born with antisocial tendencies is in effect to assert the opposite, that human beings are invariably endowed with an innate leaning to kindliness, cooperation with society, and a willingness to live peaceably. Far nearer to the truth is it to maintain that human beings by and large have at birth an implanted tendency to social living, but that exceptions to this general rule must be recognized as being equally valid.

One need not accept the moral pessimism of such prophets as St. Augustine, Mahomet, and Martin Luther, who were of the opinion that man is by his very nature a perverse being and penetrated to his very core by corruption. Nonetheless, of a great many individuals throughout the ages and down to our own time, such a judgment would certainly be valid. History, both early and recent, has noted the names of an almost unlimited array of individuals who have signalized themselves as butchers of their fellow mortals on a large scale. The majority among them required for their success and survival the possession of this particular talent to an eminent degree. It requires, moreover, no great stretch of credibility to acknowledge that for each such recorded personage there have been literally thousands who have been similarly endowed with an aptitude for destruction, even though their doings brought them no similar attention and fame. In parts of Africa, we are informed, there exist leopard men, crocodile men and hyena men who, to this very day, set themselves up as imitators of these carnivorous mammals. In India, prior to their extermination by the British, there were ritual killers, called Thugs, whose main purpose was to lie in wait for and then strangle their unsuspecting victims. Beasts in human form, while not uncommon among the "emerging" nations, are by no means a rarity even among nations that have long ago "emerged," as events of recent decades have more than amply demonstrated. Inside the human species, one can discover an immense gulf between the highest and the lowest individuals. It is a gulf that transcends all racial, national, social, and linguistic distinctions. To be noted even within the same city are unbridgeable distances in respect to both culture and ethics.

That the human family, considered as one, has not entirely freed itself from the nature of those earlier beings from which it is biologically derived is a truth that peeps out from every direction. Under the evolutionary aspect, the whole of mankind may be viewed as a recapitulation of the entire animal kingdom, embracing both its higher and lower forms. From the standpoint of behavior, the worst human specimens exhibit traits that could, without much stretching of the imagination, be seen as a heritage from the less palatable members of sentient creation. Of human characteristics and reactions, not a few should be conceded as being autonomous of all environmental factors.

Those who are repelled by the idea of biology having anything to do with crime should be asked to explain the relative absence of serious delicts among females. Women, to exactly the same extent as men, live in slum areas, come from broken homes, and are brought up by stupid and drunken parents. And yet, among them, there are about one eighth or one seventh as many crimes as among males. It is surely very odd that half the population is relatively immune to influences that occasion so much downfall among the other half.

I have sought to point out that genetics and biology have a bearing on the existence of the criminal establishment. Others, to the contrary, will continue to regard the evil state of society as the only determining factor. It is my contention, however, that between these seemingly opposite standpoints there is actually no contradiction. You cannot speak of a society that is bad without at the same time implying that at least many of the individuals who compose it are bad likewise. And when you speak of individuals being that way, you can hardly sidestep the genetic factor in their makeup.

Ultimately, bad social conditions and bad humanity are the opposite sides of the same coin. A goodly percentage of men and women of all nations, races, and classes are by nature and from their very birth greedy, heartless, bigoted, and dishonest. Collectively, they are responsible for much that goes on. There are, however, no laws, certainly not human laws, to punish such people because of their unlovable traits. By the same token, ought we to condone and forgive an act of larceny or brutality merely on grounds that in his past lifetime the offender himself may have been a victim of misconduct by others?

It is indeed possible by dint of much philosophizing to reason oneself into a state of euphoria as regards crime and criminals; and by means of casuistical arguments and the use of a prescribed dialectic to undermine the reasoning of everyday living. Concerning the impact of the ultra-charitable outlook, it is not inappropriate to quote from a revered and well-remembered thinker of the eighteenth century.

> These enlarged views, may for a moment, please the imagination of a speculative man who is placed in ease and security, but the affections take a narrower and more natural survey of their object. . . . The mind of man is so formed by nature that upon

the appearance of certain characters, dispositions, and actions, it immediately feels the sentiment of approbation or blame. The characters which engage our approbation are chiefly such as contribute to the peace and security of human society, as the characters which excite our blame are chiefly such as tend to public detriment and disturbance.... What though philosophical meditations establish a different opinion or conjecture, that everything is right with regard to the whole; and that the qualities which disturb society, are, in the main, as beneficial, and are as suitable to the primary intentions of nature, as those which more directly promote its happiness and welfare? Are such remote and uncertain speculations able to counter-balance the sentiments which arise from the natural and immediate view of the objects? A man, who is robbed of a considerable sum, does he find his vexations for the loss anywise diminished by these sublime reflections? Why then should his moral resentment against the crime be supposed incompatible with them? Or why should not the acknowledgment of a real distinction between vice and virtue be reconcilable to all speculative systems of philosophy; as well as that of a real distinction between personal beauty and deformity? Both these distinctions are founded in the natural sentiments of the human mind; and these sentiments are not to be controlled or altered by any philosophical theory or speculation whatsoever.[24]

THE THEORY OF THE SICK CRIMINAL

Failure of the United States in its welfare program to achieve what might have been referred to as "the great leap forward" is apparently responsible for the diagnosis of the sick society, and for the corollary opinion that society is itself to blame for all the "dissent" and "loss of faith" within its confines. Now, there are less stern critics who, not entirely receptive to this concept of a pestilential society, have adopted an alternative approach in their search for a nonpunitive solution to the reign of violence and larceny. It is no longer the society but the criminal who is held to be sick.

That robust English jurist, Lord Justice Goddard, who had

[24]David Hume, *An Inquiry Concernng Human Understanding,* Liberal Arts Press, New York, 1955, pp. 110–111.

no sympathy whatever for the notion that every offender is a patient, declared at the time of his retirement in 1958 that "the age-old causes of crime are still the desire for easy money, greed, passion, lust, and cruelty." To assert that being greedy, lustful, or cruel necessarily entails being sick is the beginning of a new argument over words. It adds nothing to our intelligence when we are told that buying stolen goods, trading in narcotics, and defrauding creditors are all disease symptoms.

The mysterious and nameless ailment that is said to afflict all those who stray from the beaten path has no visible origin. Its victims complain of no symptoms, nor are their day-to-day activities in any way hampered. Although all diagnostic factors remain inscrutable, the so-called sickness is nonetheless believed to be curable. The murderer, the bandit, the counterfeiter, and the swindler can all be healed of that which ails them. All that is required, according to a prominent and experienced member of the San Francisco bar is renunciation of "legal revenge" in favor of "charity, understanding, and the mood of forgiveness."[25] This formula, variously phrased, is common to all anticapitalpunishmentarians—"It is high time we took some heed of sensible twentieth-century attitudes towards what we do to those who commit criminal offences in this country."[26] A writer in a London newspaper has in similar vein recommended "the study and treatment of penological problems in the light of medical, legal, psychological and sociological problems involved."

It could be suggested , by way of commentary, that all this twentieth centuryness could be excessively costly and more than the taxpayer could afford. A Royal Commission of Inquiry appointed by the government of the Province of Quebec, and known as the Prevost Commission, was critical of the system under which "some ministers of justice get a large budget to build maximum security institutions but devote ridiculously small sums towards probationary services and rehabilitation services." Prison inmates, with insignificant exceptions, have

[25]J.W. Ehrlich, *A Reasonable Doubt*, World Publishing Co., New York.
[26]David Macdonald, M.P., House of Commons, January 26, 1966.

been exposed since childhood to the influences of the various school systems which are accessible to all at no cost and which are maintained at great expense by the public exchequer. Perhaps the majority has likewise had some religious upbringing. In the case of these enemies of society, all this has apparently been wasted. We are told that in their case, something over and above what is given to the law-abiding citizen is required. There is already the tremendous expense to the state in maintaining up-to-date prisons, with their improved accommodations, their recreational facilities, their chaplains, and probation officers. All this, we are asked to believe, is still insufficient. In order not to be deprived of some potentially "valuable assets to society," we are to provide the perpetrators of shocking crimes with some additional facilities. We are to provide them with some specially devised and delectable environment suited to their needs, or else place them inside some highly select hospitals for specialized attention by experts. Is the taxpayer to be expected to tolerate all such costly amenities, when at the same time there is insufficient money for paying proper salaries to policemen and firemen who daily risk their lives on our behalf, or for accommodating in hospitals sick persons who have violated none of the decencies of civilization?

Detention of offenders, we are told, should have as its main purpose their rehabilitation and conversion. In a disillusioned age such as this one, all sorts of people are ready and eager for new illusions. There is an illusion that persons can be cured of their criminal propensities through the ministrations of psychiatrists. Most of the federal penal institutions in both Canada and the United States presently retain the services of either a psychiatrist or a psychologist. The task of brainwashing has been entrusted to a group of professional men who are expected to be endowed not only with the necessary learning but with a degree of persuasiveness and magnetic power vouchsafed to no ordinary prison chaplain or other prison official. It is certainly not the fault of psychologists and psychiatrists that far too much is expected of them; nor are we by reason of their failures to lose our respect for their training and usefulness. The extravagant belief that terrorists and habitual spoilers are susceptible of being changed into new men has not, be it noted, been encouraged by psychiatrists themselves. As a body, these men are known to be in substantial agreement that for the majority of prison inmates, even the less hardened, the probability of induced character changes is small indeed, and is contradicted by all experience.

Not a few of the obstacles which prison psychiatrists must contend with are by their very nature insuperable. Since the prisoner thus to be won over is allegedly a victim of an unjust society, what is there in such a person that stands in need of correction? It is society that needs to be corrected. We are thus thrown back upon a social and political problem. Since bad social conditions are supposedly the underlying cause of the man's aberrant conduct, there is in fact nothing that needs to be done, beyond the mere overhauling of the social structure itself. Otherwise, the task of bringing about some alteration in his outlook and character is from the very outset a hopeless task.

It is the convict who has a grievance against society for its supposed partiality to the rich, its want of opportunities for the poor, its racialism, its inequalities. So long as there are apparent no fundamental changes in these shortcomings, not all the psychiatrists in the world will, given the lapse of two or five or ten years, bring about any fundamental change in this man's view of himself as the victim, and of the rest of us as his oppressors. The man with a grievance against society will enter prison with this grievance. Since prior to his release society is not likely to have changed itself to any great extent, he will leave it with the same grievance. He will continue to accept as his guiding principle the complaint of the prisoner about whom Oscar Wilde wrote: "Society is really ashamed of its own actions, and shuns those whom it has punished, as people shun a creditor whose debt they cannot pay."[27] It is difficult to

[27] Oscar Wilde, *De Profundis*.

discover what a whole battery of psychiatrists can do to overcome this sentiment, short of promising their patients to do everything to have society undergo some vast process of expurgation.

The matter is even further bedevilled by the fact that not a few of the psychiatrists and psychologists are themselves committed to the dogma of an unrighteous society. Their scientific knowledge impregnated with ideological preconceptions, the efforts of these men can be said oftentimes to resemble those of the student who spent many years trying to understand the eccentricities of the magnetic needle, only to realize in the end that he had all the time been peering at it through a pair of steel-rimmed spectacles.

The struggle for the soul of the redeemed offender is at best an endless battle against contrary influence. To isolate him effectively from harmful contacts with his fellow inmates would require for him a place of detention almost all to himself. Things are not helped any by the well-known aversion of prison administrators and guards, a negative evaluation that, it can be reasonably supposed, is amply reciprocated.[28] Also, the "understanding and mood of forgiveness" towards the prisoner inside the prison walls are not likely to be duplicated by the general public upon his release. Prisons might possibly be converted into places of geniality and friendliness; but creating this kind of atmosphere outside would appear altogether a chimerical undertaking.

The exaggerated hopes in rehabilitation have utterly disregarded any *proportion* between the ability of the practitioners and the triumphant results awaited of them. Such unmeasured confidence has indeed been painfully corrected. According to the well-known psychiatrist, Dr. Karl Menninger, thirty percent of the graduates of what he calls "correctional prisons," and in some areas seventy-five percent, are reimprisoned

[28]T. E. Hazelrigg, "An Examination of the Accuracy and Relevance of Staff Perceptions of the Inmates of Correctional Institutions," *Journal of Criminal Law and Police Science,* Chicago (1967).

within five years, and usually for more serious crimes.[29] There are said to be in the United States at the present time about one million juveniles, who at one time or another have been before the juvenile courts. Now, the sole purpose of these courts is to reclaim and not to punish. To the extent that these wayward youths have gotten into trouble as a result of their unfavorable background, one might anticipate such negative influence to be effectively counteracted by a process known to make the utmost use of special techniques. These correctional efforts have not been noticeably successful. In their recent book *Delinquents and Non-Delinquents in Perspective,*[30] two well-known experts on juvenile delinquency, Dr. Sheldon Glueck and Dr. Eleanor Glueck, tell what happened in adult life to over 400 youthful offenders, whose later careers they followed. Of 438 such delinquents, no more than about 20 percent avoided arrests between the ages of 17 and 25. Many became multiple offenders, and were arrested for homicides, sex crimes, and robbery.

Lady Wooton of London, writing after an experience of thirty years as both magistrate and social worker, has this to say of efforts at rehabilitation. "It is a depressing story. Admittedly, the picture presented by criminal statistics. . .may be somewhat distorted. But there is very little reason to believe that the distortion is in the direction of underestimation. And the gloom is not dispelled by the discovery that the harder we try, the less apparently do we succeed. Penal treatments could be described as cumulative failures." [31]

IN DEFENSE OF RETRIBUTION

The entire question of imprisonment as an instrument of law enforcement would appear less frustrating if a more realistic appraisal were adopted, coupled with the abandonment of all perfectionist ideals. There is "the honest generation" who

[29]Karl Menninger, *The Crime of Punishment,* Macmillan Co., New York, 1969.
[30]Harvard University Press, Cambridge, Mass., 1969.
[31]Lady Wooton, *Crime and Criminal Law,* Stevens, London, 1963, p. 2.

would declare a "war against hypocrisy." How often, we are reminded, do we unfeelingly send poor wretches to fill up our prisons, while at the same time those of us who are apparently without sin are guilty of such lapses as filing incorrect income tax returns, disobeying traffic regulations, failing to declare to customs things purchased abroad? Would not Jesus, were he to return to our midst, admonish us by saying, "Let him who is without sin cast the first stone"?

It is indeed true that few of us are entirely without sin. But sinful though we may be in some respects, the choice still lies before us either of allowing every cutthroat and pillager to go unpunished by reason of a transcendental delicacy of feeling, or of continuing to live under a rule of conduct inconsistent with the ideal, but highly essential nevertheless. The issue would seem to be one of choosing between some degree of hypocrisy on the one hand and a large dose of anarchy on the other.

And what, by the way, is meant by "hypocrisy"? Does it mean that as adults, laden with cares and responsibilities, we are no longer as morally spotless as on the day that we left the school or university? It is probably true that we are not, by and large. Does it also mean that having forfeited claims to total innocence, we no longer have any right to insist on the observance of certain norms of conduct? No suggestion could be more ridiculous. The term "hypocrisy," assuming that it has any real meaning, is a form of inconsistency in one's thinking and attitudes. Inconsistency is a common enough human failing; but one that is not excessively open to censure.

Still another objection to the imprisonment of criminals is the failure of prison inmates to reform their way of life and to become useful members of society. Our reformatories do not reform, we are told; graduates of penal institutions drift back into careers of crime, and no amount of good will or knowledge will persuade criminals to turn over a new leaf. Disregarding for the moment the obvious retort that this negative evaluation is only partially in accordance with the facts, one is prompted to suggest two imaginary alternatives for dealing with those who fall afoul of the law. They could all be freed and permitted to go on doing as they please, or else they could all be hanged or mutilated as was the practice in earlier times. Confronted with these stark alternatives, most of us, including the most ardent critics and reformers, would have no option other than to adjust our thinking to some approximation of the existing system, despite its obvious shortcomings.

Imprisonment as a form of punishment is of comparatively recent date, and moved into first place only towards the middle of the nineteenth century.[32] During the Middle Ages, the setting up of convict establishments on a scale adequate for coping with the criminal population was a practical impossibility. There was simply no money, besides which the management of prisons was not understood. The only means that they could think of for disposing of the unsocial was either exterminating them or else mutilating them and then letting them go. Imprisonment as a punishment for crimes, other than those subject to the death penalty, seems to have become fairly common during the time of the Cromwell dictatorship. The length of imprisonment was in the beginning limited to three years. This was long enough. The prisoner who was able to survive it must have been an exceptionally robust specimen. We are informed that pickpockets were "to be burnt on the left hand and to abide at hard labour in chains in the workhouse by a space of three years, and to be whipped once every month, and not to be released until restitution made to the parties injured treble the value, and whenever released to have a collar of iron riveted about the neck to be seen, and if found without the said collar of iron and convicted thereof to suffer death."[33]

The foregoing lapse into the historic should not be taken amiss, since it helps to portray all too tragically the condition of prison bondage in many parts of the contemporary world. Nothing of a quantitative nature is known of prisons and prisoners behind the Iron Curtain and within the Muslim world. It

[32]Lionel Fox, *The English Prison,* Routledge and Kegan, London, 1952, p. 16.
[33]Stephen, *History of the Criminal Law of England,* vol. 2, p. 210.

can be surmised, nonetheless, that prisoners who do manage to secure their release are far less likely than their colleagues on this continent to court the possibility of a renewed internment. This being the case, this barbaric penal system enfolds within itself an effort at rehabilitation that is, shall we say, a qualified success; and that without the aid of any psychiatrists. No one among us would care to see a duplication of this kind of success; and yet its lesson is worth going over.

I would like to dwell on this important point. The punitive aspect and the accomplishment of rehabilitation are in the thinking of many reformers considered to be mutually exclusive. This is far from being the case, however. Both these attributes, far from being in contradiction, are in fact intertwined and inseparable. Always allowing for the consideration that the protection of society and the safety of the innocent should be the predominant care, it would be safe to assert that the imposition of a penalty by a court of law carries with it the hope that correction of behavior will follow as a matter of course. It is a fallacy to assume that a mild sentence is necessarily more "educational" than one that is severe. More often than not, a controlled and moderate degree of "vengeance" is the proper road to the abandonment of the criminal mode of life. For the subduing of lawless instincts, a stiff sentence could be highly salutary and result in a new respect for authority. Possibly in most instances, an ill-advised display of clemency will arouse not contrition but disdain. There is no reason to assume that the purveying of home comforts as incidental to prison life will have a more telling effect than the home comforts to which the offender is already accustomed. In the case of middle-class offenders, such customary amenities are not likely to induce any sorrow for past misdeeds; while in the case of others who have not been used to them, the impression created can be equally negative.

The strained and unreal distinction between punishment and rehabilitation could result in some disconcerting examples of inequality of treatment. In the case of a socially prominent and well-educated embezzler, revenge can result in a brief or attenuated sentence. Such a person does not, as a rule, stand in need of psychiatric treatment. He knows all there is to know about the differences between right and wrong. In the case of some ignorant and stupid pilferer, on the other hand, the process of psychiatric care, if seriously undertaken, might necessitate his incarceration for many years. Whether the loss of a man's liberty is in pursuit of "vengeance" or whether it is motivated solely by "charity, understanding, and the mood of forgiveness" is not likely to make much of a difference in the end.

There is still one other point to be made. The equation of punishment and reform is incomplete without a third component, namely, that of deterrence. By concentrating too much on the relative merits of punishment and rehabilitation, it could be forgotten that while neither is a perfect answer, the possibility of incurring a jail sentence should act as an effective dissuasion. A numerous if indeterminate body of potential or borderline offenders is in fear of both its moral obloquy and its physical discomforts. A judge once remarked, "Judicial penalties are a warning, just like a lighthouse throwing its beam out to sea. We hear about shipwrecks, but we do not hear about the ships the lighthouse guides safely on their way. We have no proof of the number of ships it saves; but do not, for this reason, tear down the lighthouse."

THE LAW'S INSUFFICIENCY

For the defeat of rehabilitation, no small share of the blame has been cast upon the insufficiency of the laws. Such is the view enunciated in a judgment delivered early in 1968 by the Supreme Court of the state of Utah, and concurred in by all five of its justices. I quote their opinion in part: "The prime requisite towards a good relationship between a prisoner and his rehabilitation is his acknowledgment and acceptance of the fact that he has done wrong, and a realization on his part that society is his benefactor, trying to improve his lot so that he can become a useful citizen. It is difficult to supervise a man who is looking for loopholes through which he may escape from the results of his criminal tendencies. Each time he is let out on a technicality, he believes the court is on his side and so he does not have to conform to any standard, except that which he sets himself."[34]

It is my intention in the chapters that follow to enter into some examination of these loopholes and technicalities. I conclude this part of my dissertation with the reflection that where these loopholes and technicalities are abundant, criminal lawyers are correspondingly resourceful and triumphant. It is of course farthest from my intention to rob these "attorneys for the damned" of the prestige that is their due. Were it not for their skills, a vast number of inoffensive persons would be daily exposed to malicious prosecutions, as was the case of old. But thanks to their ingenious labors, a host of predatory "underdogs" are likewise being given their clearance. Let it be noted incidentally that these lowly canines have, by and large, proven themselves to be not ungenerous to their redeemers. An average emolument of some $200 an hour over a period of many years was the happy lot of one of the more notable.[35]

A certain criminal lawyer, practicing in the United States, has defended as many as 500 persons accused of homicide, obtaining an acquittal in every instance.[36] Of another it has been reported that in the course of forty years, he has served as defense counsel in at least 1,500 capital cases; and that by his own count a mere 64 were sent to jail, and only one was executed.[37] You may comb the lists of celebrated criminal lawyers in England, France, and elsewhere, and you will discover no such duplications of unalloyed success. In the United States itself, there is no shortage of able attorneys specializing in civil and commercial cases. But even the best of these are far from winning all their cases. Such feats are reserved only to those practicing before the criminal courts. Why?

[34] *Dyett* v. *Turner*, 439 Pacific Reports, 2nd, p. 266.
[35] *Time*, March 21, 1969, p. 50.
[36] *Esquire*, February 1968, p. 122.
[37] *Time*, March 21, 1969.

CHAPTER 4

The New Liberalism

ACCORDING TO A PUBLIC OPINION POLL TAKEN IN 1968, fully seventy percent of the population of the United States was of the belief that throughout the country there had been a diminution in law and order by comparison with five years earlier. Figures on serious crimes during this intervening period leave no doubt whatever about the correctness of this impression. The alarm presently uppermost in the minds of so many people is founded not so much on sociological speculations about "root causes" as on the aggravation of a social malady well beyond what is normally supportable. That is the main concern. A recent editorial in the *New York Times* stated, "Problems of criminal law. . .are not separable from changing attitudes towards race and the rights of the poor." In what way the various easements and immunities pronounced in favor of known desperadoes have helped to further the interests of the poor and of the racially disadvantaged remains an unexplained mystery. The logic here involved is on a par with that of the man who purchased an ox in order to be sure of having good cream. Throughout the length and breadth of the North American continent, it is doubtful whether there is to be found a single honest citizen, black or white, rich or poor, who has in any way benefited from the exoneration of known gangsters on "constitutional grounds."

To those who are habitually crying out about the rights of the poor, it might be suggested that they direct their solicitude to those hundreds of thousands of modest homes that year by year are stripped and dishevelled by thieves, and despoiled of their small treasures and precious mementoes. From those intellectuals, who are seized with the problems of the higher civilization, an occasional tear might be looked for over the savagely mutilated bodies of victims and their mentally ravaged kinfolk.

As with the quixotic attempt of a half century ago to elevate the morals of the nation by cancelling the sale of spirituous liquors, a similar efflorescence of disorder has been the aftermath of the more recent blanket cancellation of the death penalty. The interrelationship of skyrocketing crime and the New Liberalism is too consistent to be waved aside; and yet this juxtaposition of easy sentences and underworld audacity does not tell the full story. There is still one other factor that must be taken into account.

It has been urged, and perhaps rightly, that a greater deterrent than the degree of severity is the relative certainty of some kind of penalty being imposed. Hence, altogether crucial to any discussion of law and order is the effectiveness of the means for bringing wrongdoers to justice. It is both relevant and imperative to bring into prominence certain of the legal prescriptions currently relied upon for distinguishing between guilt and innocence, rules which can be said to lie at the very core of the administration of a society dedicated to justice.

Between the so-called systems of criminal law, such as the Common Law of England and North America, and the laws of continental Europe, which are remotely traceable to those of the Roman Empire, there is in substance almost no differentiation, all being founded on identical moral precepts. They are founded on the recognition that there is much wickedness in the world; and are intended one and all to act as barriers to the triumph of wickedness. This is undeniable. For setting these basically uniform laws in motion in specific instances, some momentous variations are to be acknowledged, nonetheless. Most critical within this area are the rules of evidence, the virtuousness of trial by jury, and the degree of latitude allowed the defense of insanity.

In an age in which all things once held in veneration have become subject to fresh criteria, certain of these traditional procedures which I now canvass could bear with some reassessment. Their possible faltering in a time of rapid change might, in Shakespearean phraseology, "make a scarecrow of the law." They might well constitute a fountainhead of needless and avoidable tragedy.

It is one of the stock arguments of anticapitalpunishmentarians that the threat of the death penalty is an empty threat and frightens no would-be murderer. While this reasoning is a seeming contradiction of the common experience of mankind, it has some potency and is not to be dismissed out of hand. Much depends on the character of the legal system. Where justice is swift and inexorable, the threat of a hanging or an electrocution can be formidable and most frightening, perhaps even too much so. Where, on the other hand, the administration of justice under what is known as "due process" has developed into a system of interminable delays, of excessive respect for technicalities, endless motions, appeals from appeals, then the prophylactic effect of any kind of penalty becomes illusory and is only to be derided. "Many holdup men might be deterred from future criminal action if they believed that our criminal justice system is swift and sure. I don't know anyone who believes that today."[1]

THE FIFTH AMENDMENT

An encyclopedic knowledge of the past would be essential to render full justice to the bizarre procedures that have been made use of by the law courts of all ages and in all countries for the purpose of differentiating between guilt and innocence.

[1]Patrick V. Murphy, an administrator within the U.S. Department of Justice, as quoted in *U.S. News & World Report,* November 11, 1968.

Among such rules of procedure, not a few have been illustrative of the dictum of the seventeenth-century philosopher Thomas Hobbes of Malmesbury, that the privilege of absurdity is one to which no earthly creature is entitled except man himself. Formalized and petrified rules of evidence, ranging from the various types of ordeal to laws governing electronic eavesdropping, have dominated criminal proceedings to this very day. Most conspicuous among present-day curiosities of criminal jurisprudence is the rule about self-incrimination, established for English-speaking countries and later enshrined in the Fifth Amendment of the United States Constitution.

The Fifth Amendment, as interpreted by the federal courts, has gone further than the corresponding rule in England in affording succor to the penitent from the perils that await him. By the Supreme Court, this rule about self-incrimination, in the words of one of its critics, "is treated with almost religious adulation."[2] In a seemingly endless endeavor to protect a defendant's "constitutional rights," the application of the Fifth Amendment has in recent years been pressed far beyond anything that ever went before. In a variety of ways, almost too numerous to mention, the virtue of silence in an accused criminal has been treated as inviolable. Often, though not invariably, it has been held that under the rule of self-incrimination an accused may not be called upon to produce documents connected with the matter of which he is accused.[3] The Fifth Amendment was successfully invoked before the Supreme Court by a lawyer in danger of disbarment for unethical conduct when he refused to produce documents relating to his professional conduct.[4]

Whenever an accused of his own accord chooses to enter the witness box to give evidence in his own behalf, the rule of self-incrimination still continues to operate in his favor. He is entitled to present his testimony in such manner as to limit the right of the prosecuting attorney to question him under cross-

[2]Justice Henry J. Friendly, in a speech at University of Cincinnati Law School.
[3]For a lengthy discussion of this question, see M. S. Wilder, "Privilege Against Self-Incrimination," *American Criminal Law Quarterly* (Autumn 1967).
[4]*Spevak* v. *Klein,* SCR (1967), p. 625.

examination.[5] Neither the judge nor the prosecution in addressing the jury may in any manner comment on the defendant's failure to testify.[6] Section 4 of the Canada Evidence Act provides likewise that omission of the person charged to testify shall not be commented upon by the presiding judge.

The rule that an accused person cannot be compelled to accuse himself or bear witness against himself is embodied in the Latin maxim, "Nemo tenetur se ipse accusare." It is not of Roman birth, however. Its origin is the Common Law of England in its early formative period; it was apparently first emphasized in the early sixteenth century. In 1537 the archbishop of Canterbury, at the instigation of the lord chancellor, Sir Thomas More, summoned to his palace John Lambert for an inquisition into his religious beliefs. Lambert was called upon to answer on oath to forty "articles" or charges. Framed as questions, these articles were calculated to expose Lambert's doctrinal convictions. Lambert's reply was that since there was no formal accusation against him, he would take no oath and answer no questions on the ground that "no man is bound to accuse himself." Lambert was soon after tied to some wooden posts at Smithfield and roasted alive. The rule thus fruitlessly invoked by the unhappy Lambert was a humane rule, and for its time constituted an important landmark in that it represented for the first time a moving away from the inquisitorial type of justice. The inquisition, or inquest, was an extraordinarily fertile and versatile device. It was a cunning method for snooping into people's affairs or opinions by calling upon them to answer embarrassing questions, while at the same time, keeping them in the dark as to what it was all about. As an instrument of the church for rooting out heresy, and of the king for establishing his authority over suspected persons, its effectiveness was so complete that it was adapted to every type of judicial offensive.

Criminal proceedings even as late as the eighteenth century were in violent contrast to those of our own time. The adver-

[5]Wigmore, *On Evidence*, 1961, pp. 2277–2278.
[6]*Griffith* v. *State of California*, U.S. Reports 609 (1965).

sary trial with its built-in safeguards for the accused was entirely unknown. Not only was the accused presumed to be guilty, but the decision against him was from the very beginning of the trial virtually assured. Under the Roman rules of procedure as practiced on the Continent, he was not even allowed to call witnesses in his favor. In England, where defense witnesses might occasionally be listened to, they were not permitted to be sworn, so that the effectiveness of their testimony could the more readily be discounted. So far as the prosecution was concerned, there were no inhibitory rules of evidence. Any kind of gossip or malicious hearsay was respected as valid and had some bearing on the outcome. Often enough, evidence hostile to the accused was presented not by the witnesses appearing in person, but by written deposition, thus allowing no possibility of any cross-examination. Any question raised as to the sanity of the accused was held to be totally irrelevant. Juries were easily intimidated and misled, and were even subject to fine and imprisonment if they did not bring in the verdict demanded of them by the presiding judge. Appeals were of course unknown.

Down to about the middle of the eighteenth century, an accused was not permitted to have a counselor represent him, but had to conduct his own defense to the best of his ability, and under the most unfavorable conditions. There were numerous rules and maxims that sound very strange to our ears, all intended to bear harshly upon the accused. He was of course not exempted from the obligation of answering all questions thundered at him by a hostile judge and a rancorous prosecutor. Almost invariably the judge and the prosecutor were one and the same person, or else substituted one for the other. As a rule the presiding judge was wont to talk rather than to listen. Part of his job was to badger the accused, to exhort and to rebuke him, and to shower him with threats and sarcasms.

Now in an age when the baiting of an accused man or woman was standard procedure, the rule against self-incrimination represented a concession, however slight, to dignity and fairness. Leonard Levy in his very able study entitled *Origins of the Fifth Amendment* gives numerous examples of persons in the prisoner's dock refusing to answer on the ground of self-incrimination, and of being upheld, even by such misbehaving judges as Jeffries and Scroggs.[7] That such refusal to answer ever saved anyone is more doubtful, however. When a certain Francis Jenkes was initially examined by the Privy Council in order to discover the circumstances surrounding his offensive remarks against King Charles II, he insisted on remaining silent under the rule of self-incrimination. The king, who was present, observed, "We will take that for an answer." No attempt was made to wring an answer out of the accused man by torturing him, as would have been the case in France, for example. But his refusal to speak was taken, naturally enough, as an indicator of a bad conscience.

Among European nations, England led the way in developing a system of justice that permitted an accused person, whether guilty or innocent, to defend himself with some chance of success. It was a gradual and tortuous process. A significant turning point was the overthrow of the despotic Stuart dynasty towards the close of the seventeenth century. As narrated by Professor Levy, "The administration of justice became dignified, decorous, and humane, so that circumstances provoking a need to claim the right against self-incrimination substantially diminished."

"At the same time," he goes on to relate "another development in the law contributed to the same end. The principle of disqualification for interest which emerged first in civil cases gradually extended to criminal cases, rendering the accused incompetent to be a witness in his own case. Anyone having a personal stake in the outcome of a trial was thought to be so irresistibly tempted to perjury that his testimony was regarded as untrustworthy. No one could have a greater stake in the outcome of a trial than the party criminally accused. It was therefore the rule that he was to be totally excluded from the witness stand."[8]

The new rule went well beyond granting a defendant the

[7]Leonard Levy, *Origins of the Fifth Amendment*, Oxford University Press, New York, 1968.
[8]Levy, *Origins*, p. 324

right not to answer. It also outlawed the right of the prosecution to question him at all. Commenting upon this reinforced privilege, a celebrated nineteenth-century jurist and political reformer was moved to declare, "If all the criminals of every class had assembled and framed a system after their own wishes, is not this rule the very first which they would have established for their security? Innocence never takes advantage of it. Innocence claims the right of speaking and guilt invokes the privilege of silence."[9]

Bentham in 1827 might have gone a step further in his denigration of a rule that was indefensible not on one ground, but on two. The guilty, who had every incentive to keep silent, were indeed fortified and protected. The innocent, on the other hand, who might be bursting to tell their side of the story were, prior to the year 1848, effectively barred from doing so. One can only speculate on the huge number of innocent persons who in the course of a century and a half were thus railroaded to their doom through being unable to open their mouths in their own defense.

Towards the middle of the last century, the enormity of this bifurcated roadblock came to be acknowledged in part. The law was amended to permit an accused person to testify on his own behalf if he chose to do so. But this concession served all the more to highlight the basic absurdity of the remaining impediment. Lord Brampton, a judge of that period, wrote of the time when prisoners were first permitted to take the witness stand and to expose themselves to the shattering effects of hostile cross-examination. He relates how on one occasion he had about come to the conclusion from the evidence of the prosecution that a man before him was guilty; but that he was obliged to change his opinion after listening to what the accused had to say. His conclusion is worth quoting. "It must be apparent to everyone, learned and unlearned in its mysteries, that no evidence can be of its highest value, until sifted by cross-examination. I was always opposed to this process as

[9]Jeremy Bentham, *Rationale of Judicial Evidence*, p. 131.

against an accused person, because I know how difficult it is under the most favourable circumstances to avoid the pitfalls that a clever and artistic cross-examiner may dig for the unwary. It did not occur to me in that early discussion of the Bill that a really true story cannot be shaken by cross-examination, and that only the false must give way before its searching effects."[10]

The observation of this wise jurist was in effect a corollary to what was said earlier by the renowned Jeremy Bentham; also to the Jewish law of Jesus' day "Nicodemus saith unto them: . . . Doth our law judge any man, before it hear him, and know what he doeth?" (John 7:50, 51). The ancient Jewish rule that no man may be condemned unless he be first given the opportunity of being heard, is nowadays a right basic to every civilized country. But by the same token, is it not implied that the man about to be judged has the correlative obligation to make himself heard, once given the opportunity of doing so?

There is nothing intrinsically irrational in the rule, "Nemo tenetur se ipse accusare." On the contrary, it constituted an important landmark in the humanization of the criminal law, and was an example that many nations were all too slow in following. It was the farfetched extension of this rule that ultimately caused it to become irrational and absurd. When, in addition to its original simplicity, it was ordained that the prosecution in its turn could not even question an accused or make any comment in open court on his refusal to testify, it was then that Common Law and common sense became estranged one from the other.

Why is a defendant in a criminal prosecution exempted from having to take the witness stand? There is, of course, an answer; but it is not a good one. There is always a danger, we are told, that even an innocent defendant on cross-examination will become confused, make an error so damaging to himself that it will cast suspicion on his entire defense. That a simple-hearted and unsophisticated person could be so confounded

[10] *Reminiscences of Sir Henry Hawkins, Lord Brampton*, Edward Arnold, London, 1904, vol. 2, p. 231.

by an aggressive cross-examiner that he would unwittingly incriminate himself through sheer fright has no validation. A witness is judged not only by what he actually answers; his entire demeanor is taken into account likewise. The man who has not been treading the path of crookedness and has nothing of a criminal nature to conceal is not often likely to lose his countenance under a system of controlled and well-regulated questioning. It has never yet been shown that men with the simple bearing of innocence have become so entangled that they have metamorphosed their innocence into guilt. Common sense would inform us likewise that the hardened and experienced bank robber who in court refused to open his mouth was not reduced to silence because of some nervous infirmity, but only from a fear of being exposed.

Each witness, without exception nowadays, is greeted on taking the stand not only by a lawyer who may be hostile or unfriendly, but also by one who is sympathetic. He is examined, not in secret, but in the presence of an audience and of his own lawyer, and very often by a judge who is neither friendly nor hostile. If heckled or badgered, he is not unprotected. Assuredly, there are limits beyond which an impartial judge will not permit any witness to be deliberately cowed or confused, by those who are without conscience, and eager to win a conviction by whatever means.

In a civil action, often involving a large sum of money, the defendant whose peril may well be equal to that of one entangled in a criminal proceeding enjoys no immunity from being forced into the witness box by his antagonist. As much human damage can result from an onslaught in the civil courts as in the criminal courts, and sometimes more. A petty thief who may be subject to an imprisonment of a few months is protected from having to testify, whereas a businessman in a civil suit for damages, who is in peril of being mulcted for many thousands of dollars and perhaps being ruined, enjoys no such advantage. Libel can be judged under the civil law as well as under the criminal law, as everyone knows, but more often nowadays under the civil law. Under a civil proceeding, the penalization, though expressed in purely monetary terms, can be more savage than it might have been in the criminal courts. Nonetheless, the defendant finding himself in a quandary of this nature has not the privilege of preserving a stony silence.

Has anyone thus far, in Canada or in the United States, disputed the constitutionality of customs and immigration officials' opening baggage of returning tourists, as well as immigrants, and asking searching questions about their previous activities and past whereabouts? And yet, such proceedings are undeniably inquisitorial and invite answers that might well result in self-incrimination.

Nowhere outside the Common Law orbit has this preposterous device for shielding the guilty been embraced, or even mooted. In Scotland, France, Holland, Belgium, Scandinavia, Italy, West Germany—in every civilized European country—an accused person is immediately taken before an investigating magistrate following his arrest, by whom he is questioned. Should he refuse to answer, he is neither punished nor threatened; but the fact is, his refusal is duly noted and commented upon at the proper time. Nowhere has it been alleged or discovered that under this European system innocent men have been made to suffer. In England, itself, there is apparently a dawning recognition of there being something phony in the untouchable tradition. In 1967 a report, "The Interrogation of Suspects," was drawn up by an influential nonpartisan organization of British lawyers.[11] In the Preface it was stated as follows: "Without any dissentients this committee has reached the conclusion that the time is ripe to abolish the privilege of the accused to keep silent before his trial, while at the same time safeguarding him from improper pressure from over-zealous police officers."

The Committee proceeded to recommend more specifically that once a person has become a suspect, he at once be brought before a magistrate who alone should have the right to question him. By way of a preliminary, such magistrate would be ex-

[11]Justice Committee on Evidence, 1 Criminal Law Reports 3155, London (1967).

pected to address the suspect somewhat as follows: "If you are brought to trial it may tell heavily against you if you have refused to answer the questions which I am about to put to you. On the other hand, the answers which you will give could clear you of all suspicion, so that you will not be brought to trial at all."

THE EXCLUSIONARY RULE

Permission finally given to an accused person to defend himself actively, whenever he chose to do so, marked the final stage in his liberation from the duress of the inquisitorial system of trial by imputation of guilt. The continued evolution of the judicial process has since been tantamount to a swinging of the pendulum to the opposite extreme. Almost a century ago, it was observed by Sir James Stephen that the defendant in a criminal action was in a far happier position than was a defendant in a civil suit.[12] In a civil action, the defendant is required to put in a statement of defense, admitting, denying, or explaining every material fact alleged against him. He must declare the documents in his possession relevant to the matter, give discovery to his antagonist, and answer interrogatories. In short, long before the actual hearing of the contestation, the defendant is compelled to disclose much of his case. A prisoner charged with a crime is subject to no such drawbacks. On the contrary, the preliminary hearing before a magistrate could be a great advantage to him as it invariably reveals at least some of the evidence that will be used against him, and often enables his defending attorney to prepare a surprise or two for the prosecution.

Let us now focus some further attention on the several stages by which the lot of an accused, at one time that of a presumed outlaw and pariah, has been raised to the presently revered and sheltered status of "underdog." "My early experience of a trial conveyed the idea that it was a formal preliminary to

[12]Stephen, *Criminal Law,* vol. 1, p. 506.

passing sentence upon the accused who had the effrontery to plead not guilty. No doubt was entertained of his guilt, but it was necessary to make the jury realize it. Gradually, but completely, a revolution has taken place in criminal trials. A new spirit now prevails in criminal courts, an anxiety to grasp and expound the accused's defense has taken the place of the confident incredulity of his having a defense at all."[13]

Regarding this "new spirit," a weighty example is the recently matured process known as the exclusionary rule, labelled as "one of the peculiarities of the American system of justice." In principle, it is the rejection as evidence of all tangible objects taken by the police in the course of searches deemed to have been carried out in an unfair manner and in violation of the Fourth Amendment of the Constitution. Among such "tainted" articles have been books of account, office files and records, firearms and other weapons, capsules of narcotic drugs, smuggled merchandise, stolen goods, marked money, bottles of liquor. Premises held to having been violated included not only homes, but also offices, hotel rooms, automobiles, and even vacant buildings in some instances. The ultimate in this mellowing process of prisoner exoneration was reached in 1967, when it was ordained, "Once it is recognized that the Fourth Amendment protects people—and not simply areas—against unreasonable searches and seizures, it becomes clear that the reach of the amendment cannot turn upon the presence or absence of a physical intrusion into any given enclosure." It was held accordingly that electronic eavesdropping and wiretapping were likewise a violation of the Fourth Amendment.[14]

In an article entitled "Illegally Obtained Evidence,"[15] one may find a compendium of rulings in which under the supervisory powers of the various appeals courts persons convicted by juries were given their freedom. I am unable to refrain from

[13]Edmund D. Purcell, *Forty Years at the Criminal Bar*, T. Fisher Unwin, London, 1916, p. 39.
[14]*Katz* v. *United States*, 389 U.S. 347.
[15]*Law Review of the Catholic University of America*, vol. 2 (1968).

citing two examples of such ultra-modern justice, drawn from a news report, and typical of many to be found in the daily press.

A man who had been sentenced to life imprisonment by a court and jury in North Carolina for rape and assault was liberated by the Supreme Court of the United States on the ground that a rifle, which had been used as evidence against him, had been taken from his grandmother's home during a search declared to have been illegal. On the very same day, the court likewise freed a certain Johnny Sabbath of Los Angeles, found guilty on a narcotics charge, on the ground that the federal officers who had entered his home in order to make the arrest had failed to introduce themselves prior to crossing the man's threshold.[16]

Not a few such happy endings have been recorded in both the press and the official law reports. Some years ago, however, a discordant note was struck by the New York Court of Appeals, giving what proved to be a short-lived victory to the reactionary forces of law and order.[17] Following the apprehension of the defendant on a minor charge, the officer making the arrest had entered the man's room, searched it diligently, and come upon a blackjack. There followed a conviction on the charge of unlawful possession of a weapon. The Court of Appeals held that even though a search contrary to the rules might expose an officer making it to the suit of an aggrieved person, the evidence so uncovered could be used nonetheless. "The question is," said Judge Cardozo on behalf of the court, "whether the protection of the individual would not be gained at a disproportionate loss of protection for society. . . . We are confirmed in this conclusion when we reflect how far reaching in its effects upon society the new consequences would be. The pettiest police officer would have it in his power through overzeal or indiscretion to confer immunity upon an offender for crimes the most flagitious." Of this particular jurist it was written, "He is not a bit sentimental about criminals. Their fre-

[16] *New York Daily News*, June 4, 1968.
[17] *People* v. *Defore*, 242 New York 13 (1926).

quent attempts to escape punishment by calling the court's attention to immaterial flaws in indictments and to technicalities in the rules of evidence left him unmoved."[18]

The reason commonly offered for a rule that constitutes a departure from wise and sober calculation is that the liberation of the criminal serves as a lesson to the police to act with more care. "The underlying rationale of the exclusionary rules is protection of the general public from police misconduct."[19] In effect, such protection to the general public has meant releasing to that public over the years a plentiful harvest of thieves, hoodlums, labor racketeers, dealers in narcotics, and swindlers whose guilt in each and every instance had been proven beyond the shadow of a doubt. To punish or admonish the police, it was deemed necessary that the public be burdened as well. The underlying peril to society inherent in this crippling philosophy has not failed to draw a warning from a member of the judiciary: "The justification most frequently offered by the courts when the accused in a specific case goes free—that it is a caution to the police to behave differently—should be carefully scrutinized. . . . The extent to which police officers see the courts as their opponents or enemies is alarming. No system can long function with this kind of conflict, where people will follow devious routes to frustrate one another. In such a situation there can be no winner, and the loser is the public."[20]

The Fourth Amendment provides that citizens are to be secure in their persons, houses, papers and effects against unreasonable searches and seizures. There would have been no subsequent agony had this amendment made clear that searches and seizures were not to be branded as unreasonable when they resulted in the incrimination of public enemies; and that the mere infraction of rules, in the absence of bad faith, was not to serve as a pretext for transposing guilt into innocence. On the stone facade of the Criminal Courthouse in the

[18] Joseph P. Pollard, *Mr. Justice Cardozo,* Yorkton Press, New York, 1935, p. 61.
[19] *Terry* v. *State of Ohio,* 392 U.S. (1968).
[20] Judge William T. Downs, "Wanted a Balanced System of Justice," *Crime and Delinquency,* New York (April 1969).

city of Montreal is engraved the following legend: "Frustra legis auxilium quaerit qui in legem commit." Translated, this means that it is useless for anyone to expect aid from the law when he is himself a violator of the law. It is a valid deduction that a culprit ought not to be encouraged to turn the tables on those who brought him to justice. There is no reason in the world why he should be allowed to gain from any carelessness or want of discretion on the part of his captors.

On the question of searches, the French Code of Criminal Procedure pronounces as follows: "Searches shall be effected in any place in which may be found objects, the discovery of which may be useful to the manifestation of the truth" (Article 94). Subsequent articles of the same code then proceed to enunciate rules for the proper conduct of such searches, as well as other police procedures. To those neglecting any of the safeguards thus insisted upon, Article 136 contains the following notice: "Failure to observe the formalities prescribed for warrants of appearance, attachment, confinement, and arrest is sanctioned by a civil fine of fifty new francs. . . . It may give rise to disciplinary sanctions or to an action for denial of justice against the examining magistrate or the prosecuting attorney. These provisions shall extend . . . to all measures protective of individual liberty." Unlike Canadian and American law, French law decrees a penalty for its custodians, both high and low, who contravene regulations in the matter of searches and seizures. But, at the same time, it refuses under any such circumstances to impair public security by giving known offenders another chance to resume their depradations.

THE CULT OF THE UNDERDOG

Formalists who in earlier times insisted on the letter of the law as a ground for punishing even the innocent have been succeeded by others using similar means for securing ludicrous acquittals. Evidence upon which a conviction has been based must be scrutinized not so much for the possibility of being false or perjured or weak, as for the manner in which it has been obtained. Should it be established that it has been obtained by methods that could be regarded as unsportsmanlike, the case against the convicted prisoner would be vitiated. It is then the prosecution, to say nothing of the police, that becomes the object of the court's displeasure.

The refurbished rules of evidence presently insisted upon in many of our courts, and more especially in appeal cases, with their pedantic insistence upon method, are a violation of the inherent desire of the human heart for righteousness in judgment. One may well ask how the ruling out of unimpeachable testimony, no matter in whose favor, accords with the Biblical command, "Justice and only justice shall you follow" (Deuteronomy 16:20). Let it be added, likewise, that the cult of the underdog and the veneration of the poor, as judicial postures, are in direct conflict with the Scriptural warning, "Neither shalt thou countenance a poor man in his cause" (Exodus 23:3).

The eagerness to save from punishment in the name of liberalism has given birth to a network of barricades designed for the submerging of evidence and for thwarting the conviction of known criminals. The "Warren Court" discovered fresh avenues of escape for suspected persons. The famous Mallory decision of June 27, 1957, constituted a breaking of new ground in this particular "New Deal."

In April 1954, a woman in Washington, D.C., was raped in the basement of the apartment building in which she lived. The circumstances clearly indicated that the perpetrator of this crime was one of three young men; but since the rapist wore a disguise, the woman was unable to make positive identification. The police took all three suspects to headquarters for questioning. They all agreed to take a lie detector test. At the conclusion of the test, Andrew Mallory confessed to the crime. Seven hours had elapsed, however, since he was taken into custody. The police were unable, because of the lateness of the hour, to locate a magistrate. Mallory was therefore not arraigned until the following day. For this reason alone, the Supreme Court, by majority vote, reversed his conviction, saying that the delay between arrest and arraignment was too long.

Some nine years later, in *Miranda* v. *Arizona,* decided on June 13, 1966, the Supreme Court in a five-to-four decision promulgated some new restrictions on police interrogaton of criminal suspects. The decision provided that no confession—even if wholly voluntary—could be admitted as evidence in a state or federal court unless the prosecution was able to prove that a fourfold warning of his rights had been given to the accused before he was questioned. He was first to be told that he had a right not to answer. Then, he was to be told that whatever he said could be used against him. Third, he must have an attorney at his side during all questioning. Fourth, if indigent, he must be provided with an attorney at the state's expense. The Miranda decision was an abrupt departure from precedent and upset what had been the law since the earliest days of the Republic. Justice Black, in opposing the majority decision, expressed the view—one from which it is difficult to believe that the average reasonable citizen would dissent—that "the desirability of bringing criminals to book is a far more crucial consideration than the desirability of giving defendants every possible assistance."

Perhaps even more advanced in the way of "giving a defendant every possible assistance" was the remarkable decision in the Wade case,[21] which, like the judgment in the Miranda case, was ultimately declared null and void by a vote of 51 to 31 in the U.S. Senate. By the same majority of one, the Supreme Court declared that the identification of a suspect by witnesses during a lineup was invalid since the particular suspect thus identified had not at the time been represented by counsel.

The judges of this continent, more especially those sitting in appeal, by their commitment to the technicalities of procedure, have in many instances acted as though society was made for the law rather than vice versa. It is fitting to observe, nonetheless, that members of the judiciary have themselves been outspoken critics of this trend. "No matter how atrocious

[21]U.S. Reports, 1966.

the crime or how clear the guilt, the Supreme Court never discuss in their opinions or even mention the fact that the murderer, robber, or dangerous criminal or rapist, who has appealed to their court for justice, is undoubtedly guilty; and they rarely ever discuss the rights and the protection of the law-abiding people in our country. Instead they upset and reverse convictions of criminals who pleaded guilty, or were found guilty recently or many years ago, on newly created technical and unrealistic standards made of straw."[22]

I close my inquiry into these matters by suggesting that this doctrine is ruinous to the security of the public and of the state, for it requires that justice, in seeking for the truth in matters concerning murder, treason, or any other of the major crimes, be confronted with hazards that have been artificially created. In no other fields of humanistic or scientific inquiry are there similar restraints that must be obeyed. No question has ever been raised in astronomy, or biology, or history, as to the "fairness" of any investigation or discovery.

SOME PUBLIC OPINIONS

All too frequently the moral certainty of a man's guilt is, on the part of a watchful public, frustrated and baffled as a result of fatuous quibbles that are altogether foreign to the merits of the case. Added to this are the innumerable instances of decisions being reversed by courts of higher instance by reason of a word spoken out of turn by judge or prosecutor, or by reason of a police officer failing to utter the correct formula at the time of an arrest, a search, or a seizure. No attentive onlooker could, as a result of such upsetting, be expected to alter his opinion as to the guilt of a culprit, often some notorious character, whose guilt was determined by a unanimous verdict of judge and jury, after a long drawn-out proceeding.

A word of caution is here required. Those critics who are disposed to blame the courts for the degradation of law and order do not altogether hit the mark. A habit of ill-omened

[22]Chief Justice John C. Bell of the Supreme Court of Pennsylvania, at a gathering of district attorneys in Philadelphia, July 8, 1968.

indulgence is at bottom no more than a mirror of public apathy and misguided sympathies. Judges and lawyers are hardly to be expected to show themselves more solicitous of the public safety than is the general population. The depredations of criminal elements, undoubtedly made easier by paralyzing court decisions, have been aided to no small extent by well-intentioned and not so well-intentioned members of the lay public. An inclination to look upon lawlessness as somehow akin to the struggle for civil and individual rights has as its counterpart an unfriendly posture towards the police. Accusations hurled at the guardians of the law are commonly participated in not only by lawbreakers and their well-wishers, but by politicians and do-gooders at large. The information media are full of reports, articles, and letters denouncing the police in almost all their activities, ridiculing their suggestions for improved law enforcement, and often referring to them as being themselves a threat to society. Such contemptuous rejection of men whose calling requires them to risk their very lives for the protection of society is perhaps symptomatic of an age in which all values have been turned upside down.

The philanthropic attitude towards malign individuals comes easily enough to those who have never been their victims. Because liberals are unable to bring themselves to the belief that there are situations that only the use of force can resolve, their readiness to join in the clamor about the "overacting" of the police is the more readily understandable. A just and vigorous response by the New Jersey State Patrolmen's Benevolent Association is here worth recalling. "To the commissioners and public we would like to ask one question: When a law enforcement officer, faced with the extremely dangerous task of quelling what is in fact an armed rebellion, is the target of sniper's bullets, rocks, and bottles, just exactly what constitutes 'undue force'?"[23]

[23] *New York Times*, May 17, 1968.

THE POLICE STATE

Charges about "police brutality," currently made by law violators and special interest groups, are intended for no other purpose than to slacken the intensity of response to criminal acts. Among the deceptive canards issuing from the mouths of demagogues and activists is the conjured-up fear of the "police state," having as its supposed prototype the security squads of Soviet Russia and Nazi Germany. The "police" of these two states were engaged primarily in political espionage, and were concerned exclusively with the tracking down of internal foes of the dictatorships. (Of course, the police of the Soviet Union still are.) Their role in combating crimes against peaceable citizens, such as theft and murder, was altogether minimal.

In all democratic states likewise there exist secret intelligence services for the purpose of discovering enemy agents and spies. But these are quite distinct from the police units maintained by local authorities. The latter are indispensable to any state, be it democratic or not. They might be clothed with extensive powers, such as that of holding suspects in long captivity without trial, or executing them in secret fashion. But even with such enlarged duties, they are no more than the minions of those by whom they are delegated, and cannot proceed beyond the orders given from above. States have been ruled wholly or in part by landowners, merchants, soldiers, priests, lawyers, slaves. Never have they been ruled by policemen. Hitler was no policeman. Nor was Stalin, or Mussolini, or Mao, or Brezhnev of that profession. The "police state" is a convenient term of opprobrium employed mainly by those suspicious of too much law and order.

WIRETAPPING

Second only to inept references to the "police state," the most conspicuous example of the New Morality is the frenetic outcry against "electronic eavesdropping." As a law enforcement officer, you may not listen in on the plans of suspected gangsters, extortionists, drug peddlers, conspirators, kidnappers, or spies, without first engaging in a clearing process with some higher authority. On May 27, 1969, the Canadian Association of Police Chiefs, appearing before the Justice Committee of the Canadian House of Commons, sought unrestricted power to eavesdrop electronically on suspected criminals. They pointed out that delays in getting permission in each instance from a judge enabled racketeers who had their own listening devices to complete their operations and clear out betimes.

The request of the police chiefs, we are informed, was coldly received by the members of the committee. A former university dean of law objected to a "radical change in the normal system of checks and balances." A writer who conceded that wiretapping was effective in cases of syndicated crime, systematic bombing, and various forms of conspiracy declared that to give the police open authority to take such measures "poses a dangerous principle," nevertheless. A spokesman for the Canadian Civil Liberties Union, appearing before the committee, suggested that the police chiefs were threatening to "wipe out centuries of legal history" and would bring about "a tragic shift in the balance of power within society. . . . What they are saying in effect is that they will designate who are criminals and then subject them to unlimited harassment through the medium of an electronic bug."[24]

Concepts of right and wrong do not remain entirely static, it would seem. Not so long ago, obscenity and pornography were considered salacious. Nowadays, it is a mark of superior refinement to say that you do not even know what the words mean. "Invasion of privacy" or "erosion of privacy" has now become one of the more deadly sins. Let no one be so literal-minded as to imagine that all this worry about privacy has anything to do with someone merely breaking into your home. The fear is of something far more transcendental. With long-range microphones and other secret instruments mass-produced by present-day technology, the dread now uppermost is that the more sportive among the citizenry will soon be

[24] *Toronto Globe and Mail,* May 30, 1969.

devoting many of their leisure hours to planting microphones inside the dining rooms and bedrooms of their unsuspecting neighbors, and then be listening in with glee to their table talk or loveplay. Preoccupation by solemn parliamentarians with such trivia brings to mind that censure of Jesus: "for ye make clean the outside of the cup and of the platter, but within they are full of extortion and excess" (Matthew 23:25).

Now, none of these playful devices can be considered as lethal. They are intended only for listening. And those listened to are the very people who are engaged in asserting their constitutional rights of freedom of speech. Now if something be lawfully spoken, then surely it may be lawfully heard, even by some uninvited auditor. Your right of free speech has never been so well protected as it is today. Why then seek to hinder those who wish to listen to you? You are permitted to use foul language. Does it really matter how many hear you? Under the new sex morality, it is your privilege to copulate with anybody you please. This often entails a certain amount of verbalization. Should it be made a criminal offense to tune in on your love-making? No one nowadays can stop you from protesting or in any way speaking your mind about anything. You may even go so far as to advocate the overthrow of the government by armed force, without being punished for it. Do you object to the presence of an enlarged audience while you are thus holding forth? Should you happen to be a captain of industry or a director of a company, you are no longer supposed to have any secrets. It follows that here too you have no right to complain of the bugging of your board room. Why then all this heated talk—and among our most progressive elements no less—of putting people in jail for using extrasensitive devices, when all that is needed is a little of the old-fashioned dialectic to prove that the freedom to listen is every bit as sacred a right as the freedom to speak?

But both these freedoms, in all seriousness, could do with some paring down. Where malice or subversion is involved, there ought to be penalties both for speaking and for listening. For the moronic prankster, who is not normally anxious to get into trouble, a law against "bugging" could have some effect. But for the practicing bank robber or extortionist, a warning of this nature would be no more effective than telling him that he may not carry a gun. On the other hand, if the police and other agencies of law and order were in any way restricted from using the very latest in scientific devices for the purpose of tracking down public enemies both domestic and foreign, there could be serious consequences. That such officers, in the process of seeking out their quarry, are bound to make numerous wrong turns and inadvertently overhear much that is innocuous and inconsequential should be a matter of no more than superficial regret. The exaggerated clamor notwithstanding, nothing very traumatic is likely to be the outcome from such "invasions."

CIRCUMSTANTIAL EVIDENCE

The notion is widespread among the public that there is something disreputable in what is disparagingly referred to as "circumstantial evidence."[25] As opposed to this type of proof, stress has been laid on the greater reliability of direct evidence, that is to say, the testimony of eye witnesses who claim to have been the actual spectators of the crime committed. But it has been found time and again that such evidence, when unsupported by circumstantial details, can be most fallible. About thirty years ago, John Labatt, president of Labatt Breweries of London, Ontario, was kidnapped and held for ransom. On giving his testimony in court, Mr. Labatt pointed to the accused and said, "He kidnapped me." The jury, knowing the excellent character of Mr. Labatt, believed him and returned a verdict of guilty. The man was given fifteen years. Two years later, the man who actually kidnapped John Labatt gave himself up. The mistake in identification was undoubtedly an honest one.

Experienced lawyers and judges have expressed a great deal

[25]In this connection, see the report of a book written in prison by a convicted murderer, showing his conviction to be resting only on "a tight chain of circumstantial evidence," in *Time*, September 27, 1968.

of skepticism about the testimony of witnesses who claim to having seen things. "Human testimony has been sweepingly condemned as being largely the product of distorted recollection, unsound inferences from inaccurate observation, and baseless conjecture. This stricture may be too severe; but such investigations as have been made support the view that the usual assumptions of human testimony err on the side of generosity, and that the value ordinarily assigned to it is exaggerated."[26]

Be it observed that circumstantial evidence so often impugned, through blunted insight, is simply an application of the law of causation, in the absence of which nothing of consequence would ever have been proven of anything. Men have been convicted, and properly so, on the strength of logical deductions from admitted facts; but likewise have they been saved by the exercise of the same thought process. Invariably, circumstantial evidence, provided that it is relevant, has some merit. Very often, however, it is insufficient to bring about a conviction. The inference created may be strong enough to warrant suspicion; but suspicion is not the equivalent of proven guilt.

In 1936, Bruno Hauptman was found guilty of the kidnapping and killing of the infant son of Colonel Charles Lindbergh. No one saw either the abduction or the killing of the child. Hauptman was convicted on circumstantial evidence. Yet this logical chain of circumstances was compelling in its conclusion; and after the lapse of several decades not a single thread of this powerful web has been torn asunder. Hauptman was seen in the neighborhood of the Lindbergh home at the time of the crime. Further, the ladder used in bringing down the child was proven to have been made of wood found in his attic. These facts, in themselves, were significant, and were certainly enough to create a strong possibility of Hauptman's involvement. Yet in the minds of most thoughtful people, some doubt of his guilt would have remained, had the matter rested

[26]Jerome Frank, *Not Guilty*, Doubleday & Co., New York, 1957, p. 199.

there. Such doubt had to be dispelled, however, once it was proven that the ransom note was in Hauptman's handwriting, and finally that the ransom money had been found in his possession. Even then, there were those who persisted in doubting this circumstantial evidence, among them the governor of the state of New Jersey. But their obduracy merely served to highlight the distinction between reasonable and unreasonable doubt. Men at all times have shown their proneness to err either by believing that which they ought not to have believed, or by refusing to believe that which they should have believed.

REASONABLE PREJUDICE

It is one of the crystallizations of modern justice that the accused must at all times be given the benefit of the doubt. In the abstract this is a good and tenable rule; and yet, like nearly all other imperatives, it is, in practice, not without blemish. Aside from the obvious consideration that what is doubtful to one may not be doubtful to another, and that doubt can vary according to the mood of the individual doubter, there are persons whose character and reputation are such that it could be considered highly imprudent to allow them their freedom simply because of some lingering doubt about their involvement in a major crime. Beccaria discusses the hypothesis of a suspected plotter against the state. In instances where completely satisfying proof of guilt is lacking, he recommends a course halfway between acquittal and condemnation. He recommends that such a person be kept in mild detention for at least some period of time. This would seem a wise and prudent measure in many instances and could result in no irreversible act of injustice. The wrongful detention of an innocent person can be corrected once an error is discovered. It is not usually too late to indemnify him and to restore his wonted place in the community.[27]

[27]In most countries of the free world there are now statutes that provide for compensation to those wrongfully convicted and imprisoned. In 1896, Adolf Beck was convicted of fraud by an English court and sentenced to seven years. It was discovered some five years later that he had been wrongfully imprisoned. He was awarded an indemnity

It is better, we are from time to time assured, that a hundred guilty men be acquitted than that one innocent person be mistakenly condemned. This assertion is contestable. An unjust condemnation is a defeat of justice. So too is an unjust acquittal. It is difficult to argue which is the greater evil. It would depend on the nature of the offense. Certain it is that failure to convict a murderer or a spy, later found to be culpable, is a far more serious matter than, let us say, the wrongful sentencing of a woman for theft from a store. The latter error is remediable, the former is not.[28]

The maxim that an accused is reputed to be innocent until he is prove guilty can, on occasion, be highly unrealistic, and in flat contradiction to the real thoughts of those participating in the trial. As regards the inner thoughts of those called upon to take part in proceedings against a major offender, including the judge, members of the jury, counsel, and the various court officials in attendance, three distinct attitudes are perceptible. First, there are those who enter upon their functions without any preconceived notions as to guilt or innocence. Second, are those who believe the accused to be innocent; and third, those who at the very outset believe him to be guilty.

Now at first sight it might appear that to suspend one's private judgment for as long a time as possible stands at the pinnacle of philosophical detachment. In most instances this would probably be the case. And yet a person who enters upon a controversial issue devoid of any preliminary ideas may do so because of some constitutional apathy, a failure to acquaint himself with what goes on, or an excessive preoccupation with his own personal affairs to the exclusion of all else. As regards those other functionaries of the court who get on with their duties in the belief that the accused is either guilty or innocent, it may be said of both these groups, provided they are intelli-

by the government of 4,000 pounds. In the United States, a federal law of compensation has been in effect since 1938.

[28]It has been asserted that in England since 1850, not a single person has been found to have been wrongfully executed (Richard S. Lambert, *When Justice Faltered*, Methuen, London, p. xii). In the U.S.A., where trials lasting more that three years are not uncommon, the possibility of an innocent person being finally held guilty has been reduced to almost zero.

gent and conscientious, that there is nothing wrong with either of their postures. Of both groups alike, it could be affirmed that they are "prejudiced," if by this is meant that their opinions have been formed on the basis of incomplete knowledge of the matter at hand. This is one of the commonest of all human failings, and one that must be lived with. It is not fatal so long as there is also a readiness to reform such premature views once the occasion for fuller enlightenment presents itself. The wisest among us will not be inhibited from yielding to tentative impressions about all sorts of matters, impressions that we later feel compelled to abandon as erroneous. Two examples are pertinent.

A prospective juror takes his place with the firm conviction that the defendant is innocent. So far, so good. But his state of mind might be such that nothing he hears will cause him to alter his bias. He may be by nature stubborn and unreasonable; the accused may be congenial to him by reason of religion, or ethnic origin. The presumption of innocence, sanctified by the law, is here followed so unswervingly as to become less than admirable.

Again, a prospective juror or judge, prior to assuming his judicial function, may have read in the newspapers of the assassination of a prominent statesman; and that the act in question was witnessed by scores of persons, ruling out all possibility of doubt as to the killer's identity. Should such a person be later called upon to serve at the man's trial, it is understandable that he has already formed some opinion about the blameworthiness of the act in question. He might be considered an imbecile or worse if he were not already prejudiced against the accused. Nonetheless, he is not to be disqualified on the ground that he has been in the habit of keeping himself informed about what goes on and that, like millions of others, the tragedy has filled him with revulsion. Despite what can be termed his lack of detachment, such a person might still be fully capable of listening with care to an argument by the defendant's lawyer, and in the end overcoming his initial repugnance to the accused by proof, let us say, that the accused was hopelessly insane, or that he had some legitimate and overpowering grievance against his victim.

In practice, there is no greater virtue in prematurely taking for granted a defendant's innocence than in presuming his guilt. This is not the test of the truest judicial temperament. The test is whether or not an accused person is allowed a proper trial, given the fullest opportunity to defend himself, and listened to with some degree of sympathy and understanding. What is true in practice should likewise be true in theory, as there is really no such dichotomy. The legal presumption that every person is innocent unless proven guilty is perfectly sound as regards the citizen who walks the streets in freedom and who has not been formally accused of any crime. His reputation may not be good; but so long as he is not taken before a court of law and charged with some specific offense, he is rightly held by the whole world to be an innocent person. The situation should be regarded as changed, however, once he has been formally charged with an offense, either by the police or by some aggrieved citizen laying against him a sworn charge and complaint. Such a person can no longer in sound logic be presumed to be innocent. But neither, on this account, ought he to be presumed to be guilty.

Many doubtful things in science and in business are being constantly investigated without any prior belief one way or the other. When the Defense Department in the U.S.A. is trying to decide whether a contract for a new military airplane will be awarded to the Boeing Corporation or the Lockheed Corporation or the General Dynamics Corporation, it carefully scrutinizes the plans and specifications, the prices, and delivery dates of all three competitors—or so it is hoped—but it does not commence this investigation with a presumption that one of the three has any overall advantage or superiority. And so it is with many problems in science or in business, or in medicine, or in any field where the truth is sought after. Similarly, in the case of the investigation of a crime—and a trial ought to be above all a dispassionate search for the truth—the truth may be sought after without any presumption as to where it may lie.

CHAPTER 5

The Jury on Trial

THE SIGNIFICANCE OF THE SYSTEM OF TRIAL BY JURY HAS been explored in many works of great scope and authority. As a method of symbolizing the participation of the community at large in the trial and punishment of any of its members, such trials have, in one shape or another, existed since the earliest times. It has been represented that this system of lay justice has exercised an uplifting influence on the people's sense of right and wrong. There is hardly any reason to take issue with this appraisal. As a most ancient and respected survival of early justice, the right to trial by jury has been an appendage of popular government, and has shared in its vicissitudes. In ancient Greece, the ancestral home of democracy, we discover a shape and structure remotely akin to its modern counterpart, though more closely related to it in spirit.

An Athenian jury was made up of anywhere from 200 to 2,000 members, chosen by lot from among the entire body of citizens. It was distinguished from its modern successor in that it had no presiding judge; nor did it engage in any discussion or deliberation. The contestants or the accused having been heard out, a secret vote was thereupon taken, with a verdict rendered according to the majority. Socrates was tried before a jury of 501, with a majority of 60 voting for his condemnation and death.[1] A judicial body so gargantuan was, as may well be surmised, highly susceptible to caprice and mob psychology. The unemployed, the uneducated, and the more resentful elements of the population were invariably eager to serve. And in so doing it was within their power to vent their spite on litigants who were above them on the social scale. At the same time, however, the very magnitude of the Athenian jury made it virtually impervious to coercion or bribery.

In its more familiar form, the jury can be said to have been devised in England not long after the Norman Conquest, and more specifically, in the judicial reforms of King Henry II during the middle of the twelfth century. Trial before judge and jury combined was then conceived as a compromise between the unfettered authority of the itinerant judges appointed by the king and wholly subservient to his wishes, and the parochial sentiment of the country people with an instinctive distrust for strangers coming to sit in judgment on their friends and neighbors. It seems also to have grown up as an alternative to the ordeals, and was therefore welcomed as giving a defendant at least some opportunity of proving his innocence. Even before the suppression of ordeals, it seems to have been not unusual for accused persons to purchase from the king, not exemption from punishment, but the right of going before a jury.[2] The judges of medieval and later times were in any event not of such impeccable character as to warrant their being left to themselves. Since the records that have come down to us tend for the most part to show them in an unflattering light, it was well that juries did exist, even though they were not as a rule a potent factor.

The jury system under the early law of England, while outwardly a concession to popular sentiment, was one which an autocratic and self-centered ruler could afford to tolerate. At a time when justice was prodigal in human blood, in order for its fury to be mitigated, a jury would almost invariably be obliged

[1]So outraged were the Athenians by this decision that a number of those whose votes helped to condemn Socrates were hounded into committing suicide.
[2]Stephen, *Criminal Law*, vol. 1, p. 257.

to clash with the presiding judge, who was there to see to it that the will of the sovereign was carried out. During such confrontations, insofar as knowledge of them has come down to us, it would be the judge who would insist on a verdict of guilt and the jury on one of acquittal. Rarely, if ever, was it the reverse. Most especially this conflict of judge and jury was openly displayed in the highly dramatized "state trials," in which matters of high political or religious motivation were at stake.

Until late in the seventeenth century, when an outburst of popular spirit called forth a kindling of fresh impulses, a jury which refused to return a verdict of guilty when required to do so by the presiding judge could be heavily fined or imprisoned. Juries that had the audacity to act independently, and in opposition to the Crown-appointed judge, were rather few and far between. Thus in 1670, William Penn and William Mead were tried in London at the site of the Old Bailey for preaching to an unlawful assembly at Grace Church. The jury refused to find them guilty. By way of punishment, those voting for acquittal were locked up for two days and two nights without food, and then ruinously fined for their contumely.

In the American colonies, notable exceptions to the prevailing subservience of juries to the royal will were to be seen from the very beginning. To these early settlers, there seemed no surer champion of the popular cause against the tyranny of the sovereign state than the device of trial by one's peers. Notable in the list of grievances against King George III, as set forth in the Declaration of Independence, was that of being deprived of the right of trial by jury. This right was soon to become one of the pillars of the newly created United States Constitution. Enshrined in Article III, it provides that "the trial of all crimes, except cases of impeachment, shall be by jury." As originally written, the Constitution of the U.S.A. made no mention of jury trial in civil cases. This was added, however, by the Seventh Amendment, which states that "in suits at common law when the value in controversy shall exceed $20.00 the right of trial by jury shall be preserved."

In the early nineteenth century, the English jury gained the admiration of the entire civilized world, and was installed even in Tsarist Russia; this must be accepted as proof of its underlying merit. It went into a partial eclipse, however, once its unpredictability and idiosyncrasies began to manifest themselves. Starting with the middle of the last century, there have occurred numerous breaches in the system, even in England, where nowadays no less than 85 percent of all serious offenses are adjudicated upon without jury participation.[3] Everywhere, in fact, throughout the free world, with the exception of the United States, jury trials have been drastically curtailed; this, however, would not be the place to go into any particulars regarding this matter.

On the North American continent, and in the U.S.A. especially, the fascination exerted by the jury remains undiminished. This mode of justice has in fact been able to gather new strength. In a recent decision, the Supreme Court held that the requirement of trial by jury, as laid down by the Constitution, applied equally to those being accused under state laws as well. A Negro youth convicted by a court in the state of Louisiana for striking a white boy was sentenced to imprisonment for sixty days and a fine of $150. His conviction was declared null and void by reason of the omission of a jury trial. In the absence of any line of demarcation between what constitutes a serious offense and what does not, it could be surmised that at present almost any kind of conviction within any of the courts of the U.S.A., state or federal, is susceptible of being upset should the conviction have taken place without the presence of a jury.[4]

Recently steps have also been taken to bring the jury system more into line with the ultra-democratic principles now prevailing. In a climate of opinion in which poverty and criminality are held to be more or less synonymous, it is felt that the poor should be allowed greater participation in judging the poor. Complaints have been made from time to time on behalf

[3]Sir Bernard Devlin, *Trial by Jury*, Stevens, London, 1966, p. 130.
[4]See report in the *New York Times* of September 10, 1969, regarding the decision of *Duncan* v. *State of Louisiana* (1969).

of accused housebreakers and bank robbers that in appearing before juries made up of local church wardens and presidents of chambers of commerce, they were not really being tried by their "peers." Congress has recognized the validity of this complaint by lowering the qualifications for jury service, and for securing a broader source of veniremen from among the less cultured and affluent.[5]

LAWYERS AND JURORS

Nowhere throughout the inhabitable globe has the jury as an institution had the devotion that is presently accorded to it on the North American continent. Among lawyers, especially, and apparently without much distinction as regards their place in the ideological spectrum, such ardor has amounted to almost religious worship. "Even the so-called corporation lawyer regards the jury system with too much reverence to stand idly by and see it perish in the name of efficiency, or economy or speed."[6] For Governor George C. Wallace of Alabama, the right of trial by jury is equated with freedom of speech, freedom of religion, and freedom of the press.[7] Of the late Clarence Darrow, it was said that "he knew juries are more to be trusted than judges, when it comes to the protection of the life and property of the citizen."[8] Even more pregnant with adoration is the summation of a leading trial lawyer of San Francisco, "Today the jury system is the only defense against arbitrary judges, the only defense against persecution, and the only defense against our government. In short, our jury system is the only defense of man against himself."[9]

Now the author of this encomium thereupon proceeds somewhat perversely to advise us how simple it is for a jury to be born less than immaculate. "Choosing a jury," he informs us,

[5]Federal Jury Selection Act, March 1968. See also *Time*, September 27, 1968.
[6]Joseph T. Karcher, "The Case for the Jury System," *Chicago-Kent Law Review*, vol. 45 (1968–69).
[7]*U.S. News & World Report*, October 28, 1968.
[8]See Foreword by Justice W. O. Douglas to A. Weinberg, *Clarence Darrow, Attorney for the Damned*, Simon & Schuster, New York, 1957.
[9]J. W. Ehrlich, *A Reasonable Doubt*, World Publishing Co., New York.

"can be similar to a military attack; and not even the Almighty will help the lawyer who goes into court with no clear idea of the personalities who will be sitting before him on the jury." This is indeed a truly remarkable derogation from the belief that a jury can be trusted, come what may, to defy prosecutors and arbitrary judges and to defend "man against himself." The inner wheelings and dealings that are to be followed in order that juries might serve as the perfect instruments of Divine justice they are intended to be are fully explained by this highly realistic advocate.

Experienced and conscientious counsel representing an accused will go to great pains in seeking to determine in advance the manner in which a jury most favorable to his client might be brought together, a strategy requiring the most painstaking effort, and one which the overworked prosecuting attorney is rarely in a position to emulate. Now, since the twelve men or women who are finally selected to sit on a jury must come from a considerably larger number of persons who under one set of rules or another are summoned to appear on the day of the trial, the defense attorney who wishes to succeed in both achieving a reputation and maintaining it must bend himself to the task of finding out beforehand as much as possible about the background, opinions, and habits of each of these veniremen. This task, Herculean though it may seem, has not been such as to daunt those members of the criminal bar who have created for themselves well-deserved reputations for skill and ability as defending counsel. Ehrlich, in his book, informs us of some of the decisions that must be arrived at by a defending attorney in pondering beforehand the coming struggle with his opponent, the state prosecutor. Thus, in each and every instance, thought must be given as to whether it is advisable to have on the jury a man or a woman, a white man or a colored man, a rich man or a poor man, a man with technical knowledge or an ignoramus. Ethnic origin can be of overriding importance.

Now we are not to suppose that all this finesse is idle and meaningless jockeying. It is part of the established experience of counsel who specialize in the dogged and pertinacious defense of men whom, in some instances, they know to be innocent, and for whom very often they work for little or no payment, as well as of the most undeserving and notorious professionals by whom they are paid well enough, and who constitute the lucrative part of their clientele. No censure whatever ought to attach to these attorneys for the observance of these rules of good preparation. Quite the contrary. But it must be admitted that the entire business, preliminary to the actual trial, is replete with the element of ruse and combat, and hardly at all with the spirit of high-minded and disinterested justice. The need for such tactics does nothing whatever to support the exalted view of the system of trial by jury, so lyrically insisted upon by those trained to its advantages. Quite the contrary, it does go far to explain how it has come about that so many decisions of juries have turned on irresponsible motives, such as the relative poverty of the parties, their religion and ethnic origin, and the attractive characteristics or other of the contending counsel.

A successful criminal lawyer is one who has trained himself in the art of caressing members of a jury, much as the Japanese geisha girl has been trained in the art of pleasing all men. The jury, in its turn, is apt to be greatly impressed by the tone of the advocate's voice, his display of pathos, and even, it has been claimed, by the cut of his apparel. Blazac once defined a jury as a body of twelve men chosen to decide which side has the better lawyer. Lawyers, as it happens, are greatly intrigued by the consciousness that in appearing before a jury, they are in effect themselves undergoing trial.

A very experienced, if somewhat cynical, member of the judiciary has presented us with a possibly exaggerated portrait of this highly ingratiating pleader for justice.

> A book could be written on the subject of the influence of the personality of the lawyer in the courtroom. Each workman must use his own tools, and so the lawyer must fight with his natural weapons. We have winners in all fights. There are men who walk

> into the courtroom with so much dignity and weight, who speak with such gravity and solemnity that they create for themselves a funereal atmosphere that overshadows everything. They carry an impression of such deep learning that the words they speak seem to have a tenfold weight.... Then we have the lawyer who plays the farmer, deliberately slaughters the King's English, chews tobacco prodigiously, offers his plug to the jurors and gets their sympathy and good will by appearing to be one of them, and by making it seem that their interests are common against the oppressor on the other side of the table.[10]

To a great many thoughtful observers, the inadequacies of the existing system of trial by jury have been long noticeable.[11] Notwithstanding, for the legal profession as a whole, the maintenance of its present character remains an undeviating principle. The grounds for this infatuation with the status quo I shall now endeavor to expatiate upon.

For those who have eyes to see, it should be manifest that many if not most of our professional services have come into being largely because of the inherent deficiencies of mankind's earthbound existence. Were all human beings from the time of birth until advanced old age to be blessed with unfailing health throughout their lives, there would be little need for physicians, dentists, nurses, pharmacists, hospital orderlies, and other kindred occupations. Similarly, should the era of universal peace be most unexpectedly inaugurated, so that human beings without exception were to become sedate and unaggressive, a great army of soldiers, policemen, jailors, and perhaps even trial lawyers, could be dispensed with. It is of such lawyers, and more especially of those devoted to criminal practice, that I would speak further.

Now I intend no disrespect to this profession when I assert that its membership, in common with the membership of a goodly number of other callings, has some vested interest in the world as presently constituted, complete with its present

[10]As quoted by Jerome Frank, *Law and the Modern Mind,* Anchor Books, New York, 1931, p. 183.
[11]For a full discussion of these defects, see Jerome Frank, *Courts on Trial,* Princeton University Press, Princeton, N.J., 1949.

shortcomings. Its means of livelihood would vanish overnight were the established method of settling disputes between the individual and his neighbors to be displaced. For these men, the laws and their restraining influence are matters of life and death. It should be added, however—and I speak of this only in respect to their capacity of professional men and not as citizens—that their zeal for the preservation of order is less ardent than is their dedicaton to the laws themselves. Law and order are by no means synonymous. You may have a good deal of the one and not much of the other. In Soviet Russia, there is plenty of order, but not much law. On this continent, the reverse situation would seem true. Never before on this continent have there been so many binding authorities on points of law, so many judges and so many lawyers, and all accompanied by an unremitting acceleration of crime and violence.

Now it is certainly indisputable that while a number of trained criminal lawyers are employed full time by local authorities in prosecuting offenders, their earnings taken as a whole are insignificant by comparison with the fees received by their far more numerous brethren who devote their skill and most of their time to defending persons who are in trouble. Hence, unlike his predecessors of earlier times, who were not even allowed to represent accused persons in court, the typical criminal lawyer of today is very much oriented in his thinking to the needs of the "underdogs." Now when these gentlemen, "standing between the mob and the jury pleading for sanity, reason and objectivity," theatrically warn us about the jury being "the essential bulwark against oppression and the arbitrariness of the judge," they do not actually mean to throw us into a fright by conjuring up a possible return to the bad old days of Charlemagne and Henry and James and their ruthless judicial stooges. What they are in effect telling us—though not with perfect candor—is that the jury system, as presently constituted, simply makes it easier for them to obtain surcease for their clients.

The jury's composition is often determined by which of the opposing lawyers is the more skillful. Under the system of peremptory challenges and incidental tactics, which to this very day retains somewhat of the spirit underlying the primitive trial by combat, the more experienced lawyer knows instinctively which of the prospective jurors is the more likely to favor his client. The fact that such preliminary warfare might consume anywhere from a full day to a full month does not in the eyes of the professional constitute a negative characteristic.

While juries have been known to convict when they ought to have acquitted, it is generally accepted that the reverse has been far more common, even though no means are available for establishing this statistically.[12] The laxity of juries is no recent discovery. Well over a century ago, the redoubtable Daniel Webster, who himself had a way with jurors, warned, "Whenever a jury, through whimsical or ill-founded scruples, suffer the guilty to escape, they become responsible for the augmented danger of the innocent." It has been declared by critics of the jury system that "Mr. Prejudice and Miss Sympathy are the names of witnesses whose testimony is never recorded, but must nevertheless be reckoned with in jury trials." It speaks well for the humanization of our present society that Mr. Prejudice has lost most of his influence, and is far less likely to be listened to than formerly. Cases such as the Scottsboro boys in Alabama and Leo Frank in Georgia, already quite exceptional in the early part of this century, are alien to the consciousness of our times. Mobs standing outside a courthouse howling for the blood of innocent persons have certainly gone out of fashion; forever, it is hoped.

Miss Sympathy remains a potent force. Juries are sensitive to a number of situations. They are known to be recalcitrant in bringing in verdicts of guilty whenever in their view the resulting penalty is likely to be excessively severe. Thus in the state of Minnesota, some years ago, it was found necessary to reduce the statutory penalty for arson. It was then expected that "the less severe penalties provided by this act will probably lead to more frequent convictions under arson statutes, since juries

[12]The ratio of acquittals to convictions by juries is about one to three.

will now be more willing to bring in verdicts of guilty."[13] In their study, *The American Jury,*[14] Kalven and Zeisel provide us with a number of standardized instances in which juries extend themselves to discover mitigating factors. They are known to seek very hard for excuses in behalf of those whom they consider "to have been punished enough already." Also, in the case of Negroes and Indians they have often moved to leniency on the assumption that such people are less responsible for their acts than the majority population.

A partial victory is sometimes achieved by a defending attorney when he succeeds in winning over to his view one or more of a minority of jurors who refuse to bow to the majority in favor of conviction. This is known as a hung jury and in practice is a long step towards ultimate acquittal. Such failure to achieve unanimity is relatively infrequent, but is far from unusual in trials where there are political overtones, prominent personalities involved, and where the penalty can be severe. The reform substituting majority decision for unanimity, adopted by all the enlightened nations of Europe, has thus far had no impact on this continent. It recently failed to gain approval among Canadian lawyers.

Delegates to a recent meeting of the Canadian Bar Association held in Vancouver had before them a proposal that, following the example of England and Scotland, the verdict of a jury need no longer be unanimous. The majority view was "not to strip away safeguards which have long been established by tradition." One of the delegates, John Cassels of Ottawa, informed his colleagues that of the seven hung juries that he had experienced, there were five in which the majority was eleven to one. When he suggested that in instances of indecision occasioned by a lone dissenter, bribery and corruption could be a factor, he was told in reply that "it was up to the police to be cleverer than the crooks."[15]

From the standpoint of "the bleeding hearts," trial by jury

[13] *Minnesota Law Review,* vol. 35 (1950–51).
[14] Little, Brown & Co., Boston, 1966.
[15] *Montreal Star,* September 5, 1968.

has the added virtue that verdicts of guilty, when they do happen, do not necessarily stand up. There might have been much wrangling between opposing counsel during the selection of the jury, and frequent challenges for cause, calling for the presiding judge to intervene. Hence there is often a possibility of appeal because of the jury's improper composition, as in the Witherspoon case, in which the Supreme Court of the United States in June 1968 threw out a conviction for murder and a sentence of death by reason of the jury having been a "hanging jury." The alert attorney, for all his reverence for the jury as an institution, has a cold enough eye for any deficiencies that may creep into it, and dutifully announces them to a higher court—if it suits him to do so, of course.

Jury trials are of a character that make them highly susceptible of being declared null and void by courts of appeal because of observations considered not fit for the ears of jurymen on the part of judge or prosecuting attorney. In the case of long drawn-out proceedings, this is very apt to occur. Nothing ever happens, incidentally, when the ears of the jury have been similarly assailed by a volley of irrelevancies from the mouth of the defending counsel. Verdicts are upset very frequently on appeal, not by reason of inherently faulty conclusions, but because of technical grounds. Apparently, the intelligence of the average jury and its unaided ability to weigh all the facts brought to its attention are held in such little esteem by the higher judiciary, that on the merest dropping of some careless expression by the prosecuting counsel or the judge on summing up, or on the omission of something the jurors should have been told, the jury is declared to have been "prejudiced." With that, the painstaking preparation of many weeks and the laborious gathering and taking down of evidence are brought to nought, to say nothing of the expenditure of much money by all the parties concerned. The overabundant usage of the term "prejudice" has been the clue of defense attorneys to upset verdicts arrived at without there having been any indications of fraud, lying of witnesses, or underhand tactics on the part of anyone participating.

An unnecessarily low estimate of the jury's collective intelligence and an excessive devotion to protocol have combined to make all jury trials hazardous and indecisive.

> A trial judge has now to concern himself not only with the task difficult enough in all conscience, of marshalling the evidence and explaining to the jury the law relating to the matters which have been actually in contest between the prosecution and the defence, but he has also to anticipate the attack upon his charge that may be made in the appellate court if he fails to the jury aspects of the law and the evidence which neither the prosecution nor the defence has advanced. Unreal though the whole business may seem to any but lawyers, an omission to do so may result in a quashing of conviction and an order for a new trial. Hence trials are taking longer, and judges' charges to juries are losing the desirable features of compactness and lucidity. This development may be partly explained by the failure to keep in mind the utilitarian function of the criminal law, but one suspects there are other and deeper reasons stemming from uncertainty about the validity of fundamental assumptions.[16]

There seems hardly any need to furnish concrete examples of such "failure to keep in mind the utilitarian function of the criminal law"; and yet I am unable to resist the temptation to do so. A news item of September 10, 1968, appearing generally in the world's press, provided the information that the English Court of Appeals had paved the way for the publication of a book that, it noted, contained "on virtually every page words and incidents which in the ordinary colloquial sense would be rightfully described as obscene." The Appellate Court, the report went on to relate, did, nonetheless, discover in the jury's decision condemning the book "a fatal flaw," in that the trial judge had failed to guide the jury on whether or not its publication was for the public good. In the state of New Jersey, the appeals division of the Supreme Court unanimously overturned the conviction of the Negro playwright Leroi Jones,

[16]Morris and Howard, *Studies in Criminal Law*, Clarendon Press, Oxford, 1964; from the Introduction by the Honorable Sir John Barry, Judge of the Supreme Court, State of Victoria.

convicted earlier in the year of carrying weapons during the July 1967 riots in Newark. The conviction was overturned on the ground that the charge made to the jury by the trial judge was unfair to Jones because in it the role of the police in the case was extolled.[17]

TRIAL BY NEWSPAPER

In the eyes of most lawyers, judges, and legislators, the jury system is indeed a sacred relic, especially to those who have benefited from its weaknesses. But as with all relics, it is nonetheless held by its venerators in secret and probably exaggerated contempt. This underlying distrust of the entire process and the low opinion held of jurymen as a group are perhaps well illustrated by a campaign, recently inaugurated by the American Bar Association, that seeks to limit the release and publication of crime news intended "to reduce the threat of the prejudicial effect of news coverage by strictly limiting the information that can be released by lawyers, court personnel, and the police."[18] There is no fear expressed that such discussion of criminal events in newspapers would have some damaging influence on the judges themselves, so as to pervert their view of the facts. It is with the possible effects on the minds of unsophisticated jurymen that such agitation against a free press is concerned.

Campaigns against what is called "trial by newspaper" have this in common with most changes in the law presently favored by numerous reformers. They are designed to make it harder to prosecute and easier to defend, the searching for the truth being of secondary importance. Since in the eyes of the average trial lawyer, unsure of the merits of his client, the safest jurors are the "know-from-nothing" variety, the safeguarding of their pristine ignorance is of such overriding importance that reporters of newspapers ought to be barred from certain pretrial hearings and from portions of the preliminary hearings not intended for their sensitive ears. "Juror prejudice," possi-

[17] *New York Times*, December 24, 1968.

[18] *New York Times*, May 17, 1968.

bly brought about by a premature eating from the tree of knowledge, being a major peril to the proper fulfillment of their delicate mission, it must follow as an unavoidable sequel that also the public at large must be similarly blindfolded. That freedom of the press is considered requisite to a free society, that as a rule newspaper reporting is more or less accurate, that when crimes are committed against individuals, they are likewise committed against society in general, and that the public has an interest in being informed of such matters—these considerations seem to be altogether of no importance to these zealots.

It is indeed acknowledged that the U.S. Constitution guarantees the right to a free press, as well as the right to a fair trial. But it is alleged that both these rights appear to come into conflict whenever a particularly sensational crime has been committed, and that the selection of an impartial jury is thereby made more difficult. Such alleged incompatibility between a free press and the fairness required to be rendered an accused person is largely imaginary. The mere fact that the public's curiosity or resentment of a crime has been aroused to a more than usual pitch does not of itself make impossible a just trial.

To deny newspapers the right to keep the public informed about crimes without screening, would be a form of censorship hardly less objectionable than political censorship. Even though their reports are from time to time unnecessarily embroidered, many of the newspapers avail themselves of specialized reporters, and are in fact a constructive factor. Keeping the public informed can do the cause of justice no harm. While undue sensationalism can at times inflame an irrational public response, and threaten to create a travesty of justice, their attention to the details of a trial has on numerous occasions proved invaluable. Newspaper specialists in crime have also been known to aid in the apprehension of wanted suspects. On many occasions they have also been instrumental through their own sources of information in helping the innocent person to escape unjust verdicts.

"Trial by newspaper" does not mean conviction by newspaper. It remains the duty of the judge, or the judge and jury, either to convict or to acquit. For better or for worse, news media are in some respects part of the judicial process. There can be no guarantee that publicized information will not on occasion be responsible for the gathering of rampaging mobs, the terrorization of judges, juries, and counsel, as happened in the famous Scottsboro trial in the thirties during the trial of nine Negro youngsters for rape. Likewise, owing to newspaper reports, it is dangerous nowadays to try a Negro militant for murder without arousing a threatening attitude in his followers, as happened recently in the case of a Negro agitator tried for the murder of a policeman in San Francisco and finally sentenced to a ridiculously low term of imprisonment. News media, as elements in the administration, can be either wholesome or pernicious, as can be prosecuting counsel, judges, juries, and defending counsel.

Trials carried out in an atmosphere of public excitement resulting from a blaze of publicity could be detrimental to a fair trial. This has long been acknowledged. The law does provide for a change of location of the trial, when so warranted. Notwithstanding, the positive aspects of full information provided by newspapers deserve to be emphasized, among them the revelation of the court's finding. The curiosity of the public so aroused can be most constructive and helps to underline its ultimate contribution in the process of justice. The sentence imposed on a wrongdoer by a court of law is rightly intended to inflict upon him public disapprobation as part of his punishment by depriving such a person, for a time at least, of the good will of his friends and the fraternal bonds that normally are maintained within the community to which he belongs.

It is essential that the public at large be sufficiently informed to enable it to decide whether or not the judgment of the court conforms to its expectations. But a great anomaly is here to be seen. The public, having followed the details of the trial as reported in the newspapers, has in all likelihood arrived at the same conclusion as that of the jury. Some months elapse, and there is a further report that what has been considered a fair enough decision by a jury has been invalidated by the appeals court, not on the ground that anyone had lied, or that evidence had been concealed, but solely on the ground that the prosecuting attorney in communicating his views to the jury had not done so in the approved manner. In effect, one previously held by the public to be a dangerous character is thereby pronounced more sinned against than sinning. People are then likely to shake their heads in wonder, and marvel at the vagaries of justice.

In a recent case in the Province of Quebec in which a former minister of the Crown was accused of having accepted a bribe of $10,000, a verdict of guilty, arrived at after a hearing lasting six weeks before a judge and jury, was overruled by the Court of Appeals on the ground that "in the first trial, professing to test the credibility of the accused, the attorney for the Crown had brought to the attention of the jury various matters that had no relation to the question of guilt, but might be expected to arouse prejudice against him in the minds of one or more of the jurors."[19]

In this particular instance, as in many others where a new trial is ordered, the witnesses were no longer available. By agreement between the parties, the second trial took place before one judge, sitting alone with the written transcript of the original witnesses, alone to be relied upon. The new trial lasted no more than a few minutes, and the accused was declared to be innocent, notwithstanding that of the fourteen men who participated in judging him at both trials, thirteen had found him to be guilty. In the eyes of the law this man was proven innocent, but it would be difficult to assert that he was proven innocent in the eyes of the public.

Adverse opinions on the decisions of tribunals will continue to be expressed in private, and no proposal could possibly be entertained that would make such freedom an offense. Likewise, could there be no talk of proceedings being taken against

[19] *Montreal Star,* April 17, 1968.

various law journals when they print adverse criticisms of such decisions on points of law or fact. I conclude my observations on this part of my theme by suggesting that law courts and judges ought to be no more exempt from criticism by newspapers than statesmen and legislatures are.

JUDGES VERSUS JURIES

Conditions under which juries operate nowadays differ greatly from those of earlier times. Under the English system, unlike that of ancient Greece, the jury from the very beginning was presided over and directed by a judge. Hence trial by jury is, in theory at least, a combined operation of judge and jury. In practice, the seniority in this partnership was held by the judge in earlier times, but for a long time has been usurped by the jury. The function of a judge presiding over a jury nowadays partakes of the relative impotence of all presiding officers, in democratic assemblies at least.

The judge is there to see to it that the jury does not stray too far from legal principles, since he alone decides on questions of law. In the main, he is there to decide what evidence the jury may legally listen to and what it may not. As regards the facts revealed by evidence that the jury has been allowed to hear, the jury frequently allows itself to be guided by the judge, who in all probability has listened more attentively than the average juror, and is better trained to weigh them fully. But since the judge is not permitted to sit with the jury during its deliberations, he has no means whatever of ascertaining whether or not his comments on the law or the facts have been taken into account. He must accept the jury's verdict as to guilt or innocence, even though he is convinced that the jurors have ignored his instructions as to the legal aspects, and even though he may be convinced that their weighing of the facts has been erroneous.

Jurymen are most frequently selected on the very day in which the trial is to be proceeded with. They are quickly ushered into a case, knowing nothing whatever of its essential features, and with no opportunity to familiarize themselves with the known facts beforehand. They are acquainted with neither manual nor textbook for their guidance, since none apparently exists. Many among them are intellectually incapable of handling a deluge of testimony. Some even give up trying. The suspicion has often been voiced that the verdict of the jury, which never has any grounds appended to it, can be the result of anything but calm deliberation, exchange of impressions, and final intelligent concurrence.

No investigator is permitted access to the inner sanctum of the jury room. Judge Jerome Frank reports that in 1947, two law students sought to discover at first hand how juries deliberate and decide cases. The students wanted to have a trial judge, at the conclusion of a jury trial, present to each of the jurors a carefully worded questionnaire to be answered either in writing or in the course of interviews. They made this proposal without success to nine judges in turn. One judge observed, "How they decide is their own business." Another remarked that he did not approve of any "holier-than-thou attitude towards juries."[20]

Jurymen, in the course of a trial, are from time to time sent out of the room, as though they were children, lest they listen in on arguments not intended for their ears as to the admissibility of evidence. Rules for the exclusion of evidence have been established mainly because of their reputed incompetence. Notable is the rule excluding hearsay evidence, that is to say, statements made by persons outside the court who are not available for cross-examination. Such evidence, with certain exceptions, is not allowed. Doubtless, such secondhand evidence, as it is sometimes called, ought to be treated with caution. But 90 percent of all the evidence, on which men in industry and business rely for forming decisions, is the equivalent of hearsay. Yet on account of the ineradicable belief that jurors will make no allowance for the secondary quality of such evidence, it is excluded entirely. Hence, important facts that

[20]Jerome Frank, *Courts on Trial,* p. 116.

could lead to a more correct appraisal of an issue are artificially excluded.

Now all this winnowing out of forbidden things notwithstanding, what remains in the way of admitted evidence can present a formidable enough challenge to a group of men and women whose minds are supposed to have been adequately conditioned. It seems indeed remarkable that of this same group of men and women, of whose average intelligence no very high opinion is entertained either by legislatures or by appellate judges, some really extraordinary feats are expected, nevertheless. It is expected of them that they give their undivided attention to all the witnesses throughout a long and tedious session, that their memories be unfailing as to every question and answer, that they manage to retain an open-minded attitude to the very end, that they distinguish truth from falsehood in each and every answer by all the witnesses, no matter how numerous they may be and how contradictory. Finally, and above all, in cases where insanity is pleaded and where expert testimony is presented, jurors are expected to have within themselves the ability to determine whether the man is sane or insane, a task admittedly difficult and complex. All this they are deemed capable of doing. The one and only thing that is considered to be beyond their mental powers is the relatively simple distinction between what is hearsay evidence and what is not.

Jurors cannot be prevented from realizing that there are aspects of the case about which they have been deliberately kept in ignorance. On the contrary, they have been compelled to listen to what they could well have done without, such as lying and unscrupulous witnesses, the browbeating of honest witnesses, the false emphasis on the incidental and the irrelevant, the cat-and-mouse dialectic, trifling conundrums elicited during cross-examination, and, above all, the hysterical and irrational antics of counsel.

"Few of those who listen to a lecture seem to take in more than a small proportion of the statements made by the lecturer, or even to absorb intelligently the points that he has more strenuously endeavoured to bring home. This common failure of attention is not merely due to intellectual dullness or slowness. Many intelligent and quick-witted people make a like failure."[21] The Webbs in this instance were complaining of the lack of concentration on the part of members of commissions appointed to examine social problems in which they were at the time interested. To possibly an even greater degree, such criticism should be applied to jurymen, for the most part untrained, bored, unwilling. All the more so, since the perennial exclusion of evidence, which is the incessant feature of every jury trial, can only exaggerate a situation of this kind, and the wrangling that takes place preliminary to such exclusion can scarcely improve matters.

The old-fashioned theorem that the presence of a jury is essential to the operation of justice is really a hangover from feudal times. Under a system of justice shackled by bureaucracy, pedantry, and unabashed favoritism, the jury was often instrumental in providing at least a glimmer of fairness. The times have since changed drastically; and with the changing of the times has come a totally altered judiciary. Judges are nowadays, with only rare exceptions, honest, and do not react to outside pressure. Above all, their decisions are subject to appeal. To a judiciary so corrected, the trial of most suspected persons could with safety be entrusted, without the intervention of laymen who are for the most part both untrained and reluctant to be called upon. The security that can be taken for justice, as contrasted between one system and the other, was well summarized by Sir James Stephen, a judge of the nineteenth century: "The judge is one known man, holding a conspicuous position before the public, and open to censure and in extreme cases to punishment if he does wrong; the jury are twelve unknown men. Whilst the trial is proceeding, they form a group just large enough to destroy even the appearance of individual responsibility. When the trial is over they sink back into the crowd from whence they came and cannot be distin-

[21] Sidney and Beatrice Webb, *Methods of Social Study*, Longman's, Green & Co., London, 1932.

guished from it. The most unjust verdict throws no discredit on any person who joined in it, for as soon as it is pronounced he returns to obscurity."

Since the time of the foregoing pronouncement there has indeed taken place a partial retreat from the jury system in all democratic countries other than those of this continent. In France, Germany, Holland, Belgium, and Italy, and even England, it did not take long to discover that the system of calling in juries, for matters both civil and criminal, adds enormously to the cost of doing justice. Not only must large sums be paid out to jurors and prospective jurors, but businessmen, skilled workers, executives of corporations and farmers were being called away from their customary duties, while spending much of their time sitting idly in the courthouses awaiting their summons to duty. Since the turn of the century, an immense decline in the volume of jury trials, criminal as well as civil, has taken place, so that trial by a judge alone is now the rule, and trial by jury the exception. There has been no complaint that the number of miscarriages of justice has since been increased.

SHOULD JURIES BE ABOLISHED?

I have quoted with some degree of approval the arguments of eminent authorities who have set out to show that jurymen are beset by difficulties greater than those which men who are professionally acclimatized must contend with, that their capacity for attentive listening is limited, and their ability to sift evidence rudimentary. I consider it proper that the reader should have before him a contradictory opinion, which I now quote, so that he may the more readily decide for himself which is the stronger viewpoint.

> The charge that the average juror is not competent to determine the facts, and apply the law properly is without foundation. The jurors usually represent a true cross-section of the community, of average intelligence, capacity, and virtue. They bring a fresh, alert, unbiased approach to each and every case upon which they sit. If the judge alone were to try the case there

> is no guarantee that any better grade of justice would be administered. Judges are also human. Some are weak, while others are strong. Some are emotionally stable, others are equally susceptible to emotional appeals. And while most judges are undoubtedly honest and honorable and impartial and capable, there have been some exceptional cases where a few of them have been found not to be.
>
> It would therefore appear that a composite of the intelligence and fairness and balance and dedication of the average juror is at least as good a guarantee that a correct verdict will be rendered as if the jury were dispensed with. Extensive surveys show that the collective recall of evidence and the collective intelligence of 12 jurors is at least equal to, if not superior to, the same capacities of a single jurist.[22]

In Karcher's defense of the jury system, there is to be found none of the dire predictions as to the harmful consequences of giving a lone jurist full authority to determine a matter without a jury. It is certain, however, that any criticism of the jury system becomes blunted once account is taken of the fact that all human justice, regardless of system, is beset by the imperfections of human nature. The latter part of his argument is undeniably persuasive, though. The inherent virtue in the give and take of jury discussion cannot be dismissed. In a bench trial, the evidence must be acted upon by only one man. He does not have the help of disinterested persons in exposing all the facts, in drawing correct inferences, in examining the elements of credibility, and in weighing each item of evidence. Where there are several persons, on the other hand, evidence can be scanned more minutely, each juror has the help of the other jurors in remembering what was said, in drawing attention to what is most pertinent, in pointing out errors, and in drawing inferences.

It could, of course, be argued that the potentially inflammatory discretion of a single judge could be sidestepped by the decretal of a court composed of three judges sitting together. A court so constituted would enjoy the advantages of a deliber-

[22]Joseph T. Karcher, "The Case for the Jury System," *Chicago-Kent Law Review*, vol. 45 (1968–69).

ative body without its inherent drawbacks. Such perfection might well be achieved in instances where the three judges were unanimous. Where, however, they would divide two against one, as would often be the case, this advantage would be lost. A majority of only one is not much different from a minority of one, and carries little weight. A majority of two judges to one would in all likelihood carry less moral authority than a majority within a jury of eleven to one. The participation of a substantial number of persons, be they lay or professional, does not fail to have a mollifying effect in overcoming doubt and allaying skepticism.

I make the following generalized submission on the subject of juries:

1. The adverse criticism leveled at the institution, though serious enough, is not such as to warrant its total abolition.
2. Jurors are not necessarily incompetent merely because they are uneducated. The instincts of a healthy-minded laboring man are more to be trusted than those of a neurotic or cynical doctor of philosophy.
3. There are matters of such grave moment that come up for consideration by courts of law that they cannot in good conscience be left to the purview of only one man. A judge acting alone ought not to be given the responsibility of deciding whether or not an accused is insane. When the death penalty is restored—as it is bound to be sooner or later—no civilized human being can be expected to assume the burden of deciding on a man's life all by himself.
4. All this being said, the proponents of the jury are unable to provide any defense in the case of two major defects. The time has come to correct these defects without doing injury to its substance. Hence a jury system more responsive to the needs of our time will now be proposed.

THE UNANIMITY RULE

While the mental and emotional health of accused prisoners is nowadays subjected to intense scrutiny and discussion, no such tests are applied to determine the fitness of those who far more than the professionally trained jurists are the true referees. While in the course of being questioned, the potential juror is rarely ever sworn, and no record is made of the questions put to him and his replies. He often fails to disclose facts about himself that might cause him to be biased, or that might cast some doubt on his intelligence or honesty.

It may be true that the persons so chosen represent a cross-section of the community at large. In such a cross-section, persons of sound character and sobriety of judgment will undoubtedly predominate. But a majority under present conditions is simply not good enough. Under the rule of unanimity presently in force, and maintained with great doggedness, it suffices for a single cantankerous and chronically unreasonable individual, or one bearing a load of grievances, or one that has been "fixed," to sabotage the entire proceedings. The stalling of the judicial process through the planting of a single biased juryman has recently been noted by the liberal-minded newspapermen, Messrs. Evans and Novak, in reporting the trial of a white assassin of a Negro leader named Damer in the state of Mississippi. The vote of the jury for conviction was 11 to 1; and that is how it remained to the very end. It was later discovered that the unmovable member of the "hung" jury was a member of the Ku Klux Klan. Similar instances could without question be uncovered by the hundreds.

The stern and rigid principle that a jury's verdict must be unanimous was probably laid down in the fourteenth century, and was only recently repudiated in England, Scotland, and most European countries. It is still clung to in both Canada and the U.S.A. The historian Hallam denounced it as a "preposterous relic of barbarism."[23] He saw in it an irrational exception to the truism that when twelve people are called together they are not often expected to take the same view of any disputed fact. Among the members of no other tribunal is unanimity a requirement. When appellate judges differ, the majority prevails. In cases of impeachment, a majority of one is sufficient.

[23]Hallam, *Middle Ages*, p. 262.

Decision-making bodies carry out legislation affecting the fortunes of millions by simple majority vote. Wars have been declared by scarcely perceptible majorities.

It is true that of all jury trials in the United States, and probably in Canada as well, not more than 5 percent fail to achieve a concensus and have to be discharged without having rendered a verdict. But it is quite certain, likewise, that in a great many of the others, the reported unanimity is more surface than real, and is reached only after many hours of impasse under high pressure from outside and as a matter of convenience. "The truth is that verdicts are often the result of the surrender or compromise of individual opinion. One or more jurymen find themselves in the minority, and many causes concur to render them less tenacious of their opinion than we might expect."[24]

The rule of unanimity has been defended as a safeguard against precipitancy, and as a creditable factor for obviating popular recrimination. It could be conceded that a jury decision by a bare majority would often fail to carry with it the necessary public acquiescence that gives strength to every judicial action. However, a vote that is overwhelming or substantial, such as 11 to 1, or 10 to 2, is hardly any derogation from one that is technically unanimous. Even unanimous jury decisions have not been immune from imputations of error or worse. The public is by this time well inured to the existence of individuals who as either knaves or eccentrics delight in their powers of veto and whose spiritual homeland is one of fractious opposition. The concurrence of the presiding judge in the decision of the majority ought in all such instances to be sufficient to erase whatever negative impression is created by one or two dissidents.

INTEGRATION OF JUDGE AND JURY

The supposed partnership of judge and jury is at present decidedly a one-sided affair. With an untrained group of men and

[24]Forsyth, *Trial by Jury*, Carswell, Toronto, 1876.

women rests the main burden of rendering a decision, while at the same time hardly any responsibility devolves upon the one member of the court who is professionally trained. The equivocal position of the judge and his total isolation from the jury during the course of its deliberations in effect make of the jury a "People's Court." His role is restricted, more or less, to deciding during the trial what testimony the jury may listen to and what it may not. It is hard to believe that this would make him more popular and influential with the jury. Intelligent and alert adults do not enjoy being told during the course of an investigation in which they are invited to partake that certain facts that may be connected with the truth are out of bounds.

The judge, who is undoubtedly apt to be a better listener than any member of the jury, and who is at least as competent as the more intelligent among them in weighing the evidence, has no voice whatever in the final determination. His influence on the jury is to all intents and purposes that of an outsider. He can be listened to and ignored at the same time. His direction to the jury may count for less than a stray news item or a chance editorial in a local newspaper. In his charge to the jury, which, in some respects, amounts to a marginal participation in its deliberation, he must exercise great care lest he say something or omit something that will become an issue in a subsequent appeal. For inflammatory and absurd utterances inside the jury room there are no similar tribulations.

Some acquaintanceship with the principle features of the most recently revised French Code of Criminal Procedure could be of value in the task of reassessing old procedures and pointing the way to a correction of the weaker aspects of the North American jury. Without being less humane, the French code, along with the West German, Dutch, Belgian, Swiss, and Italian codes, will be found eminently reasonable.

French penal law recognizes three classes of criminal offenses, each being tried before a specialized court and under a distinct procedure. First are the petty offenses, or *contraventions de simple police.* These are tried by a single judge sitting alone in a *Tribunal d'Instance.* The second group of offenses is the misdemeanors, or *delits;* these offenses are punishable by imprisonment up to five years. They are heard by three judges sitting concurrently in a *Tribunal de Grande Instance.* Finally, and from our point of view of immediate interest, are those offenses known as *crimes* or *felonies,* which are punishable by the most severe penalties, including imprisonment at hard labor, imprisonment for life, or death. This most serious category of offenses is tried by the *Cour d'Assises,* which holds quarterly sessions, and which is composed of three judges together with a jury of nine laymen, the latter being chosen by lot. Under the comparable West German system, the court consists of three judges and six jurors.[25]

Under both the German and the French systems, judges and jurymen, when deliberating, form a single unified panel. They all retire together, once all the evidence has been gathered; and after spending some time in joint discussion and deliberation, they vote for guilt or acquittal by secret ballot. Under the French system, in which the combined panel of judges and jury consists of twelve persons, eight are required to convict. Assuming that all three judges vote in favor of conviction, at least five of the nine jurors must so vote likewise. The announced intention is to prevent the judges who may be inclined toward severity from exerting too preponderating an influence on the result.[26] Under this proposed innovation, a more evenly balanced division of labor between judges and jurors would be achieved. The often puzzling distinction between what is fact and what is law would be entirely sidestepped. So too the need to shield lay adjudicators from certain kinds of evidence that, though relevant, are considered to be too much for them.

[25] *Bundesgesetzbuch* 1950, no. 40, sec. 522, arts. 81, 82.

[26] Pierre Bouzat and Jean Pinatel, *Traité de Droit Penal et de Criminologie,* Librairie Dalloz, Paris, 1963, tome 2, sec. 1083 *et seq.*

CHAPTER 6

The Defense of Insanity

I HAVE ENDEAVORED TO POINT OUT THAT THE DEFEAT OF law and order has stemmed from the abolition of the death penalty, and secondarily from the gaping loopholes in criminal administration. I now enter upon the third and final portion of my saga of the breakdown of justice. Remaining to be treated in connection with the trial of offenders is the plea of insanity, a topic of the highest practical importance. The stimulus behind much of this interest and discussion is the relative ease with which felons have been able to convince judges and juries that their mental condition has been such as to entitle them to escape responsibility for their actions.

It has been affirmed that the plea of insanity is raised in not more than two percent of all jury trials.[1] Taking into account the more recent developments surrounding this issue, this would seem a somewhat low estimate. Be that as it may, the matter is far from peripheral. The actual ratio of such trials to the total number is no criterion of their significance. Murders are not less material because they are under two percent of all indictable offenses. In terms of averages, the number of lawbreakers is even today only an infinitesimally small number

[1]Rita James Simon, *The Jury and the Defense of Insanity,* Little, Brown & Co., Boston, 1967, p. 8.

compared with the entire population. Trials turning upon the question of the sanity of the accused, if relatively few in number, are distinguished nonetheless by their inordinate costliness, their length, and sensationalism. Almost invariably, nowadays, the question of insanity is raised in trials following politically motivated assassinations, or where the accused happens to be a person of consequence, or of high social standing.

It could of course also be argued that the doing away of the death penalty, and the abatement of all other penalties, has tended to make less expedient a defense founded on a plea of insanity. Moreover, even acquittal on this ground does not carry with it an automatic return to freedom.[2] Nonetheless, confinement in a mental institution is even today often a welcome substitute for the rigors of a penitentiary; all the more so since it is certain to be of relatively short duration. "The indefinite commitment at the discretion of the Lieutenant-Governor, without benefit of statutory or other review, is not in keeping with present values and the dignity of man."[3] Some key figures in this respect could perhaps be furnished by the District of Columbia, where a recent study has shown that of those charged with murder, and later acquitted because of insanity, about sixteen percent manage to regain their freedom within five years or less. The maximum stay for all and any supposedly insane offenders seems to be eight years. Presumably by that time, the worst of these supposed lunatics are considered to have come back to their senses and no longer to require treatment. However, sad to relate, of those released as "cured," about one third do commit further crimes.[4]

ORIGIN AND DEVELOPMENT

The defense of insanity was recognized a long time ago. "Actus non facit reum, nisi mens sit rea" was a maxim enunciated by the Church in the Middle Ages. Its meaning in simple English

[2]It would perhaps be appropriate to consider such verdicts a third alternative to conviction and acquittal.

[3]K. B. Jobson, "Commitment and Release of the Mentally Ill under Criminal Law," *Criminal Law Quarterly*, Toronto (February 1969).

[4]Simon, *op. cit.*, pp. 207–208.

is, the act that is unwarranted is not to be judged as a crime unless the intention to commit such an act be present as well. A wrong committed unintentionally is not a wrong that is punishable. This salutary and rational principle is of course founded on the law of Moses. In Deuteronomy 19:4–5 it is written, "And this is the case of the manslayer, that shall flee thither and live: whoso killeth his neighbour unawares, and hateth him not in past times. As when a man goeth into a forest with his neighbour to hew wood, and his hand fetcheth a stroke with the axe to cut down the tree, and the head slippeth from the helve and lighteth upon his neighbour that he die. He shall flee into one of these cities and live."

The distinction between causing a death deliberately and bringing it about accidentally must at one time have been difficult for most people to comprehend. Otherwise it would not have been necessary for the unhappy killer to take to his heels and run for the nearest city of refuge. Some eight centuries before Moses, the Babylonian lawmaker Hammurabi had decreed: "If a physician operate on a man for a severe wound with a bronze lancet and cause the man's death; or open an abscess in the eye of a man with a bronze lancet and destroy the man's eye, they shall cut off his fingers." Even at this early stage in man's civilization we apparently discern some easement, however tenuous, in favor of one who killed without malice aforethought. The good king Hammurabi must have realized that there would have been no rush to attend the medical schools of that day without some kind of immunity granted to the unsuccessful practitioner, who while barred as a result of some mishap from the further exercise of his profession by the loss of his fingers, was still left with enough life in him at least to be able to beg for his livelihood. Under the Mosaic law, the principle of lack of intention when a killing was committed was well settled and in all probability was followed in later centuries to some extent at least. It should be noted, nevertheless, that there was not in the law of Moses, nor in any other code of antiquity, any specific mention of insanity as a ground of exemption from punishment.

Now if we penetrate to the full depth of the *mens rea* rule, we shall find it applicable to cases of insanity as well as accident. The canonical rule concerning absence of evil intention was, to the credit of English justice, accepted as early as the reign of King Edward I (1272–1307), though apparently for no offense other than homicide. The insanity had to be complete and unequivocal, and fully discernible to the untutored eye.[5] Down to the nineteenth century, the rule of insanity was thus strictly interpreted. Writing on the subject late in the seventeenth century, Lord Chief Justice Sir Matthew Hale distinguished between two forms of insanity, total insanity and partial insanity. He defined total insanity as "absolute madness" and as a condition in which the victim is "totally deprived of memory and reason." He regarded as partial insanity a condition in which the victim retained some vestige of awareness of his surroundings. Sir Matthew knew of no psychiatrists; but it could be assumed that even nowadays neither professionals nor laymen would object strongly to his distinction between insanity that is absolute and a milder form that could be described as relative, even though, as with all differentiations, difficulties must be allowed for as regards borderline cases.

An episode of the writer's own experience during his practice at the Montreal bar could serve to highlight this distinction. A veteran and highly respected member of the fire department received a severe blow on the head while fighting a fire. On being discharged from the hospital some days later, it was immediately found that his character had changed so drastically that he had to be discharged from the force. Some weeks later, the police, on a suspicion that something was wrong, broke into this man's dwelling. They saw him seated on a chair, in a trance. Nearby on the floor was a bloodstained baseball bat. Going into the bedroom, they discovered the bodies of his wife and son, lying in their beds with their skulls battered in. This man was without hesitation held to be totally

[5]Persons nowadays found to be in that extreme condition are no longer even put on trial.

insane. Had it transpired, by way of hypothesis, that instead of venting his frenzy by means of a nonlethal article lying at hand, he had gone downtown, purchased a rifle, concealed it while biding his time, killed at the opportune moment, and then disappeared, an element of planning and purposeful thinking would have entered into the matter. His insanity, while still not in any doubt, would have been considered no more than partial. For the courts of our own day, though not for those of the eighteenth century, the matter would have been difficult.

Beginning with the eighteen hundreds, hesitatingly at first, and later on with increasing frequency, partial insanity was successfully invoked before the courts of England as well as elsewhere. In the year 1800, a badly crippled war veteran by the name of James Hadfield was indicted for high treason for attempting to assassinate King George III, who by that time was himself completely demented. Defended by the famous Lord Erskine, Hadfield—who saw himself as the savior of the world—was acquitted on grounds of insanity, even though the prosecution argued that since he had been able to purchase a pistol and ammunition, there was some indication that he was not "afflicted by the absolute privation of reason." It was generally conceded at the time that Hadfield's acquittal by the jury was induced by the sight of his pitiful physical condition rather than by any departure from the narrowness of the old law.

A turning point away from the ancient practice did, however, come some years later in the famous case of McNaghten. In 1843, Daniel McNaghten assassinated Edward Drummond, secretary to Prime Minister Sir Robert Peel, in the mistaken belief that the secretary was the prime minister. McNaghten was under the delusion that the prime minister was responsible for financial and personal misfortunes that had been plaguing him through many years. This delusion was undoubtedly insane; but there were no indications that he was deranged in other respects. The jury, with the encouragement of the bench, found the defendant "not guilty on grounds of insanity." Queen Victoria, the House of Lords, and the newspapers of the day did not conceal their indignation over this acquittal. The

House of Lords thereupon called upon the fifteen judges of the Common Law courts to respond to a series of questions on the law governing insanity. Lord Chief Justice Tindal, who had presided at the McNaghten case, and who by that time apparently had some qualms about his charge to the jury, which had resulted in McNaghten's acquittal, answered for his fifteen colleagues.

The celebrated "McNaghten Rules"—under which, incidentally, McNaghten himself ought not to have escaped—confirmed, to begin with, the traditional practice of accepting total insanity. It was laid down that "it must be clearly proved that, at the time of committing the act, the party accused was labouring under such a defect of reason from disease of the mind, as not to know the nature and quality of the act he was doing." To this extent, the rule thus insisted upon differed in words but not in meaning from that expressed a century before by Mr. Justice Tracey, who declared, "In order to avail himself of the defense of insanity a man must be totally deprived of his understanding and memory, so as not to know what he was doing, no more than an infant, a brute, or a wild beast."[6]

Now in their lordships' enunciation of the law of insanity as it stood towards the second half of the nineteenth century and subsequently, the narrow medieval rule would have remained unaltered, despite the fluke McNaghten decision, were it not for the closing proviso, "or if he did know it, that he did not know that he was doing wrong."

This indeed constituted a departure in the direction of partial insanity. The terrain of partial insanity in its relation to criminal law, littered as it has been of late by the novel and abstruse terminology of the psychiatrists, was thus quite some time ago rendered untidy by this legalistic conundrum about right and wrong. Even under the very limited permissiveness of the McNaghten Rules, there was during an entire century that followed no want of casuistical debate and hairsplitting.

Where, indeed, is there to be found a human being—assum-

[6]Trial of Edward Arnold, 16 Howell's State Trials 695 (1723).

ing his mind retains a modicum of consciousness of reality—who is not called upon several times a day during his waking hours to differentiate between what is right and what is wrong? An infant six months of age already knows full well that what he receives is right and what is refused him is wrong. The editor of the Soviet daily *Izvestia* knows that what his government wants is right and what other governments want is wrong. The thief who enters your room in a motel and appropriates your wife's jewelry knows that it is wrong for her to retain such useless baubles, when they could be converted into ready cash that he himself could well make use of.

The answer that has been given to such criticism is that the appended clause about right and wrong was not meant to provoke philosophical disputation, or to encourage each and every individual to set up his own standards of right and wrong. Its intention went no further than that of stipulating the existence of a capacity for sharing in a commonplace social evaluation of a number of recognizable acts and restraints. Plainly expressed, it means this: when a person commits a wrongful act, and is at the same time aware of what he is doing, there is still a remote possibility of his being under a delusion that what he is doing is not wrong but right.

In theory, at least, the McNaghten Rules remain to this very day the basic test of the defense of insanity almost everywhere throughout the English-speaking world. Thus, the Criminal Code of Canada incorporates the answers of the English jurists almost verbatim. Section 16 reads as follows:

1. No person shall be convicted of an offence in respect of an act or omission on his part while he was insane.
2. For the purpose of this section, a person is insane when he is in a state of natural imbecility or has disease of the mind to an extent that renders him incapable of appreciating the nature and quality of an act or omission or of knowing that an act or omission was wrong.
3. A person who has specific delusions, but is in other respects sane, shall not be acquitted on the ground of insanity, unless the delusions caused him to believe in the existence of a state

of things that, if it existed, would have justified or excused his act or omission.

4. Everyone shall, until the contrary be proved, be presumed to be and to have been sane.

EXTENSION OF THE INSANITY RULE

The rule as to partial insanity, as laid down by the English justices following the McNaghten case, has since been assailed as not having gone far enough. While no attempt has been made entirely to erase the distinction between the complete and the partial prostration of the mind's powers, it has been contended that in general the human mind is weaker than was at one time supposed. Advances made in the medical branch of psychiatry have revealed it as being a complexity of motives and mechanisms; and it should be anticipated, accordingly, that it is highly susceptible of breaking down and acting explosively. The conclusion is drawn that responsibility turns not upon knowledge, but rather on the ability to monitor one's actions. A person might know that what he is doing is wrong; and yet ought to be exempted from punishment should it be shown that his wayward act has resulted from complete or diminished loss of control.

A new and far more liberal criterion for evading responsibility in cases of partial insanity, known as the Durham Rule, was adopted in the District of Columbia as a result of a decision laid down by the Court of Appeals.[7] Under this broadened and permissive formula, an accused, even though sufficiently sane to know what he was doing, and even to know that what he was doing was wrongful, was still to be exempt from punishment if he was able to prove that his unlawful act was the product of mental disease or mental defect.

A writer in the *Columbia Law Review*, commenting on this case, has pointed out, "It seems from the trend of recent cases . . . that when a defendant introduces psychiatric evidence supporting his claim of insanity, the prosecution must present

[7] *Durham* v. *United States*, D.C. Cir. (1954).

contrary evidence to avoid an adversely directed verdict."[8] The judgment in the Durham case held, in effect, that once some evidence of mental disorder was introduced on behalf of the accused, the presumption of sanity ceased. Thenceforth the burden of proof was on the prosecution to show, and beyond a reasonable doubt, that the accused was sane. The effect of the new deal favoring a more receptive attitude towards pleas of insanity was startling in the extreme. The number of acquittals by juries on grounds of insanity rose at least tenfold between 1954 and 1961.[9]

In response to the sentimentality of the times, the Parliament of Great Britain by the Homicide Act of 1957 introduced the defense of diminished responsibility. This pertains only to the charge of murder and operates to reduce the offense to manslaughter. The penalty for manslaughter in England is life imprisonment, which in practice is an average of about nine years.[10]

The new defense, we are informed, "has enjoyed remarkable success." It has been calculated that in the first twenty-seven months of its operation it was raised in seventy-three cases and succeeded in fifty-three of these, and that "juries have shown no reluctance to find that a defendant is suffering from diminished responsibility."[11] A graphic instance was that of Byrne,[12] who strangled a girl while under the influence of virulent sexual desire.

More and more has the mental institution been substituted for the house of correction; and even where least expected—in the Soviet Union, where the Bolshevik regime, when it suits its purpose, has its critics declared insane. Traditionally, this defense was available to none other than those charged with murder; but it was later extended to those involved in lesser felonies as well, such as treason, housebreaking, assault, for-

[8] *Columbia Law Review*, vol. 58 (1958), p. 1260.
[9] For comparative figures, see Simon, *op. cit.*, pp. 203–204.
[10] P. J. Fitzgerald, *Criminal Law and Punishment*, Clarendon Press, Oxford, 1962, p. 139.
[11] *Ibid.*, pp. 140–141.
[12] 1960 2Q.B., 369.

gery, and incest.[13] More recently still, have minor offenses, such as those connected with alcoholism and drug addiction, been permitted to fall within the same rubric.

No longer, nowadays, is it left entirely to the discretion of the defending attorney to raise the question of his client's mental capacity. Nor is the question of deciding who is sane and who is not a matter left exclusively for the jury to settle. By deciding whether or not an accused is "fit to stand trial," the judges have in effect taken over this question for the most part. "In Bellevue's famous psychiatric section, the prison ward has become dangerously congested as judges, grown sophisticated about ties between criminal behavior and mental instability, order more and more defendants there for observation. Last year, 1,451 persons were sent there, and scores were examined at King's County Hospital in Brooklyn."[14]

PSYCHIATRIC INSANITY

Insanity, since the time of the formulation of the McNaghten Rules, has remained a bitterly contested issue. Originally, the question of an accused's mental disorder was determined without the intervention of any medical testimony. To establish his total lack of responsibility, the evidence of the man's friends and neighbors was deemed to be sufficient. We no more require a medical man to inform us that someone is completely out of his mind than to tell us that he is without a leg, or an arm, or a finger. Only in cases of partial insanity does the polemical aspect of this question arise.

The investigation is nowadays entrusted to psychiatrists, who are deemed to be experts in detecting minute but telling manifestations of the subject's mental disorder—in the same way as the inquisitors of Medieval Europe were deemed experts in detecting religious heresy. With this important difference, to be sure: the subjects interrogated by the psychiatrists, unlike the heretics facing their inquisitors, are as a rule most

[13]The defendant in the epoch-making Durham case was charged with nothing more serious than housebreaking.
[14]*New York Times*, March 10, 1969.

eager and cooperative in aiding their interviewers, in proving that they really are afflicted with that particular malady on which so much of their subsequent safety is made to depend.

Once the sanity of the accused is called into question, the forensic struggle before the court is no longer one solely between lawyers, but one between opposing psychiatrists as well. Such confrontations are all the more natural and inevitable, since expert witnesses, unlike the common variety, are by law permitted to testify as to what they believe, and not necessarily as to what they actually know. A forensic psychiatrist called upon to examine a "psychotically disturbed" prisoner, having visited him in his place of confinement, will later pronounce him to be either a "schizophrenic paranoid" or a "pseudo-neurotic schizophrenic," depending on who called for the examination.[15] The mental expert, mandated by one side or the other, knows nothing, to begin with, of the man or his background. Like that of any other medical practitioner, his diagnosis is preceded by a questionnaire. He listens first to a recital by the patient of his "psychological troubles" and perhaps speaks as well to some of his near relations. The examination and testing are of course carried out in privacy, and free of all hindrance by the psychologist who is on the other side of the fence. Always must it be borne in mind that the questioning and reportage must not fall afoul of the rule against self-incrimination.

A mental expert, engaged by the defense, will be expected in giving his testimony to present a low estimate of his client's cerebral powers, the more derogatory the better. However, he will never be so crass as to express any doubts as to the credibility of what he has heard from either the client or his relatives in the course of his diagnosis. Contrariwise, the psychiatrist engaged by the prosecution is apt to express a lower opinion about the veracity of the man's revelations, coupled with a reasonably high estimate of his intellectual equipment.[16]

The alliance of psychiatry and advocacy has helped to make

[15]See, for example, report on trial of Sirhan, *New York Times*, April 9, 1969.
[16]For instance, the duel between psychiatrists Diamond and Olinger at Sirhan trial.

court proceedings more costly than ever. Poor men, who are frequently said to be at a disadvantage when compelled to defend themselves before the courts, are apt to suffer most of all not from lack of counsel, but from a lack of money to engage a sufficient number of psychiatrists to overtop those brought forward by the prosecution.

For every psychiatrist who will announce commandingly that the accused is insane, another will testify that he is sane; and each in his own way can be telling the truth. Hence it is not a cause for wonder that the judge in his charge will almost invariably tell the jurors that they are obliged to accept the opinions of none of them. Nor is it a cause for wonder that many psychiatrists have come to the conclusion that their proper function is that of ministering to troubled, but inoffensive, people who come to their offices. Dr. Philip Q. Roche, a former president of the American Psychiatric Association, is known to have declared, "As a man of science in search of truth, the psychiatrist has no place in the courtroom."[17] Fully thirty percent of all psychiatrists, including the most reputable, are said to refuse all employment as partisan experts at criminal trials.[18]

There is a psychiatrist who will testify that a particular accused man is insane, and there is another who will contradict him. Both opinions can be honest. There is room for similar disagreement on the more generalized plane. Not all psychiatrists subscribe to the radical theorems of their unrestrained brethren and take up an extreme position. The great majority among them are in substantial agreement likewise that very few persons regarded as abnormal are altogether bereft of the ability to plan and to reason; and that only a few of their day-to-day acts have the character of forced automatic behavior. Persons laboring under hysteria or mania are still credited with having at least some measure of self-control.

It is a well-authenticated fact that virtually all persons living

[17]Philip Q. Roche, *The Criminal Mind*, Farrar, Straus and Cudahy, New York, 1958, p. 271.
[18]Guttmacher, *The Mind of the Murderer*, Farrar, Straus and Cudahy, New York, 1960.

in civilized societies are from time to time in the course of their lives beset by emotional upsets and troubled minds. Such is the prevalence of hatred, regret, remorse, and frustration that it is doubtful if anyone can escape altogether from at times giving way to a fit of anger that could have tragic repercussions. Very few experienced and first-rate psychologists would be prepared to testify that what is really part of a normal life experience constitutes a case of insanity.

In Germany, we are informed, "there is little disagreement among psychiatrists as to what constitutes psychosis. All organic psychoses, the endogenic schizophrenias, the manic depressions, and genuine epilepsy are included. Neuroses, personality defects, and mental deficiency are excluded." The author goes on to report that on the basis of such definition of insanity, an examination over a period of ten years of 700 persistent criminals failed to indicate that even two percent were medically insane; and that in all probability if the total convict population of the Republic were to be taken into account, the percentage would be under one.[19]

It is hard not to suspect that incorporated into the supposedly cold-blooded scientific outlook of the more pompous avant-gardists is an ideological reluctance to punish criminals. To the oft-repeated allegation that the law governing insanity has failed to keep up with what is presented as the latest knowledge of the problem, many jurists have in effect responded, "So what?"[20] "While a slight departure from a well-balanced mind may be pronounced insanity in medical science, yet such a rule cannot be recognized in the administration of the law when a person is on trial for the commission of a high crime. The just and necessary protection of society requires the recognition of a rule which demands a greater degree of insanity to exempt from punishment."[21] "The pro-

[19] Dr. Herman Witter, "Psychological Study of German Recidivists," *International Journal of Offender Therapy,* vol. 12, no. 2 (1968).

[20] See Simon, *op. cit.,* for a list of some thirty decisions by state and federal courts in which the rule of the District of Columbia Court of Appeals in the Durham case is expressly rejected.

[21] *Taylor* v. *Commonwealth,* 109 Pa. State 262.

tection of society is our paramount concern. The science of psychology and its facets are concerned primarily with diagnosis and therapeutics, not with moral judgments. Ethics is the basic element in the judgments of the law and should continue to be.... We shall not blindly follow the opinions of psychiatric and medical experts and substitute for a legal principle which has proven durable and practical for decades, vague rules that provide no positive standards."[22]

All men, whether intellectuals or just ordinary people, have the inalienable right to discover whatever they wish to discover. The discovery by some ultra-liberal psychiatrists that men are not free to choose between good and evil is somewhat unfortunate; but it ought not in any way to inhibit the punishment of those who have purposely and voluntarily harmed others. "Lawyers should read not only the extremist psychiatrists who are dogmatic and aggressive in their attacks on the law of criminal responsibility; but also the works of such distinguished psychiatrists as Wertham, Cleckley, H. A. Davidson, and Norwood East, who find much merit in that law. They should ask what portion of all reputable psychiatrists in the United States are represented by the extremist critics. For example, there are approximately 8,500 practicing psychiatrists in the U.S.A.; yet the reports of questionnaires concerning responsibility indicate that no more than a handful of them have ever been consulted by members of the legal profession."[23]

INSANITY AND DECEPTION

The charlatanism in which all too frequently the plea of insanity is wrapped should embolden us to question the legitimacy of this plea, or at the very least its more radical development. The allegedly crazed prisoner often bears a remarkable resemblance to one whose lucidity is not in question. He knows when it is time to go to bed and when to rise in the

[22] *Commonwealth* v. *Woodhouse*, 164 A 2d98 Pa. (1960).
[23] Jerome Hall, "Psychiatry and Criminal Responsibility," *Yale Law Journal*, vol. 65 (1956), p. 762.

morning. He knows the proper way to dress, and to wash himself. In short, he knows all or nearly all the rules of conventional behavior. He knows likewise that when drawing a gun, it is advisable to do so when there are no witnesses; and that having done so, he must hasten his departure from the scene. Should he be incarcerated, he knows how to outwit his jailors if the opportunity presents itself.

It requires no great histrionic ability for an intelligent killer, rapist, or arsonist to act as though his mind were deranged. Holy Writ provides us with an early instance of the ease with which insanity can be successfully counterfeited. "And David laid up these words in his heart and was sore afraid of Achish the king of Gath. And he changed his behavior before them and feigned himself mad in their hands, and scrabbled on the doors of the gate, and let his spittle fall down upon his beard." The wily Judean got away with it, as we are informed. "Then said Achish unto his servants, Lo, ye see the man is mad, wherefore then have ye brought him to me? Have I need of madmen, that ye have brought this fellow to play the madman in my presence? Shall this fellow come into my house?" (I Samuel 21:12–15) David escaped from his predicament by feigning insanity; and if events run true to precedent, there have been since then many captives no less cunning, and many captors as simpleminded as the one in the Biblical account.

There is much ground for skepticism when it is claimed on behalf of an accused that he was out of his mind only at the moment of doing what ought not to have been done, but not afterwards. On the assumption that a person so unfortunate would be overwhelmed by feelings of remorse, one might expect his mind to deteriorate following such a tragedy rather than to improve. The chicanery connected with the insanity defense has provoked a raising of the colors against the entire procedure, and a veering to the opposite extreme. As far back as a half century ago, an attempt was made by the legislature of the state of Washington to outlaw all pleas of insanity. A court in that state pronounced as follows: "No defense has been so much abused and no feature of the administration of the criminal law has so shocked the law-loving and law-abiding citizen as that of insanity, put forward not only as a shield to the poor unfortunate bereft of mind and reason, but more frequently as a cloak to hide the guilty for whose act astute and clever counsel can find neither excuse nor mitigating circumstances."[24] More recently has it been written, "It is generally conceded by all legal observers that the record of the legal insanity defence is very bad, and that the softness of psychiatry as a science is at least partly responsible."[25]

The trickery and deception inherent in much of this business of insanity are highlighted by the fact that there are hardly any instances of persons wishing themselves to be declared insane until they find themselves before the court. Persons who for many years have moved among their fellow men and behaved more or less like others, suddenly become convinced by their own volition and initiative, or perhaps by those paid to represent them, that they are really *non compos mentis*, and have been so either for the greater part of their lives or merely at a critical moment.

Under the guidelines for the successfully maintained plea of insanity as already laid down by the courts, a fairly high percentage of mankind could qualify for admission into this sheltered category. By no means to be excluded are members of certain well-publicized cults, and no small percentage of "intellectuals." Obviously no follower of Mao Tse-tung, or let us say one of the student "activists," or "New Leftists," could be expected of his own volition to come forward, declare himself mentally deficient or emotionally disturbed, and request being confined to an institution. But it is equally certain that were he to find himself accused of carrying out the assassination of some "reactionary" statesman, he would spare no effort in cooperating with his lawyer, in seeking to prove his own mental deformity. The bizarre nature of his opinions would then stand him in good stead.

[24]*State* v. *Strasburg*, 60 Washington 106:110, Pac. 1020 (1910).

[25]Sandford H. Kadish, "The Decline of Innocence," *Cambridge Law Journal* (November 1968).

In no instances, other than of persons on trial for murder or other abominable deeds, are there reports of persons seeking to have themselves declared insane and in consequence confined to a lunatic asylum. It is then that the megalomaniac or self-worshipper, who has all his life believed himself to be above the ordinary run of humanity and its mores, suddenly has the urge to have himself labelled a poor, miserable and witless creature.

In all instances, where this defense is raised, there is of course no question whatever about the right man being tried, and if found guilty, about the right man being punished. However, it could be supposed that a person "laboring under a defect of reason" is capable of making a nuisance of himself by many ways other than killing, raping, and setting fires. In theory, of course, the defense of insanity is receivable in all criminal charges, small as well as great. In practice, to raise such an issue in the case of some minor infraction could be sheer madness. Instead of some light and inconsequential punishment or mere fine, a protracted incarceration in a mental institution would be risked. From the standpoint of good advocacy, there is a time to plead insanity, and a time to refrain from pleading insanity. It would hardly be the thing for an able lawyer, representing a man charged with speeding, or stealing a necktie from a department store, to start bringing up facts about his client's distorted childhood. Bringing such histories into focus would have to wait until such time as the client got into some real trouble.

It is astonishing and ironical that after an accused has been successfully steered away from a sentence in a penitentiary to one merely of confinement to a mental institution, wheels are soon after set in motion—depending of course on the availability of adequate finances—to have him pronounced as "cured." This secondary task is by no means a hopeless one, inasmuch as at the time of the trial, the "patient" had already managed to achieve a state bordering on sanity, otherwise he would not have been eligible to stand trial. Even at that time, his "psychomotor variant" or "catatonic schizophrenia," or "hypomania," or what have you, having been at its crest only at the very moment of the crime, had already been notably diminished.

Not incongruous to this part of our discussion was a decision of the United States Supreme Court in the case of *Baxtrom* v. *Herold.* [26] This decision resulted in a mass removal of inmates from two hospitals for the criminally insane maintained by the state of New York, the Dannemora and the Matteawan, to the regular civil hospitals for the noncriminally insane.[27] As a consequence, the population of the Matteawan declined from 1,523 as of January 12, 1963, to no more than 838 on September 16, 1966, the entire administrative proceeding being dubbed "Operation Baxtrom."[28] Needless to relate, the final liberation of the great majority of these "invalids" from the civil institutions to which they had been transferred was not slow in coming: and on the reasonable enough ground that as in all regular hospitals persons undergoing treatment must be sent on their way as expeditiously as possible to make room for others.

INSANITY AND CRUELTY

Extensive leeway granted to criminals on grounds of emotional and intellectual deficiencies throws light on the manner in which all amorphous concepts finally take on an important and, one might say, metaphysical development. There are now experts, including many criminal lawyers turned psychiatrists, for whom the road has seemed wide open for classifying all aggressive and antisocial behavior as symptoms of mental disorder. They are ready to assume that all such worthless and redundant creatures are "sick," and thereby discountenance all moral reflections on their conduct. Such curious discoveries are of course extreme, and constitute an attempt of theory to

[26]383 U.S. 107 (1966).
[27]Nothing has been reported as to just how welcome these dangerous newcomers were.
[28]Grant H. Morris, "An Analysis of the Confinement of Mentally Ill Criminals and Ex-Criminals by the Department of Corrections of New York State," *Buffalo Law Review* (Spring 1968).

outstrip reality. To assert that men without conscience are necessarily ill, would require acceptance of the equally absurd corollary that all decent folks are invariably healthy. It would perhaps be good news were it really true that all underworld characters, such as traders in narcotics, extortionists, and gunmen, were really in such bad condition. Sadly, however, it has to be conceded that the fellow who performs a holdup, and thereby enriches himself to the tune of $5,000, is likely to be left in a far healthier state than his victim.

Quite often judges, as well as news media, when confronted with some knavery that is more than usually revolting, are inclined to soliloquize that the perpetrator "has lost control and functions as a psychotically uncontrolled man." Ungenerous critics of such charitable hokum have insisted that this attitude has itself created a vicious circle whereby it can be argued all too speciously that the fact of the crime being sufficiently barbarous is in itself proof that the culprit was not responsible.

It seems a common trait nowadays for human beings of bland disposition to assume that characteristics opposite to their own are *ipso facto* marks of insanity. And yet it is possible for one to break each and everyone of the Ten Commandments and still be in full command of his faculties. The man who derives pleasure from witnessing another's death agonies can be as sane as the man who derives pleasure from sleeping with a woman. The many mass destroyers of their fellow men whose deeds have been recorded in history were fully as rational, if not more so, as the prophets, the philosophers, and the saints. On the contrary, the historical personalities who were in their day acknowledged to be genuinely demented, and had to be removed from their inherited functions, as happened to a number of rulers of England, France, Germany, and Spain, were mild persons and not addicted to killing.

"The harm done to mankind by psychopathic killers is enormous."[29] It should be added that the leeway granted them has

[29]Lord Taylor, president of Memorial University, as quoted in the *Montreal Gazette*, October 4, 1968.

contributed to this harm. The psychopath, who is ordinarily far from witless and well aware of the public's sophisticated naiveté, has only to plan his operation with sufficient gruesomeness to be regarded as quasi-innocent. By so going about it, he stands a good chance of convincing his judges, as well as the news commentators, that far from being a real villain, he is only "a disturbed little man with a grievance against society."

It is a safe conjecture that the Nazi war criminals hanged at Nuremberg in 1945 would have fared a great deal better had their trials taken place some twenty years later. Hitler, Lenin, Stalin, and Eichmann would have presented quite a dilemma had they now been standing to be judged before any tribunal in Canada, the U.S.A., or Britain. Since these characters were commonly designated as "madmen," it could well have been argued that their crazy escapades were traceable to "pathogenic social factors."

In a report delivered before the Magistrate's Association of the Province of Ontario, reference was made to a class of wrongdoers regarded as psychopaths, who, while not insane, are yet "unable to cope with society."[30] In his memoirs, the eminent English barrister, G. D. Roberts, Q.C., has recounted the career of one individual falling into the category of those "unable to cope with society," and with whom, it would appear, society in its turn was none too successful in "coping" as well.[31] A youth by the name of Streffen strangled three little girls in turn; but has since managed to outlive them all by a good number of years.[32] He was at the beginning charged with two victims. It was immediately shown that he had in his earlier years been certified as a mental defective, and sent to an institution from which he had been soon after released. Accordingly, the trial judge ruled he was not fit to plead on the ground that "in this country we do not try people who are so insane as not to understand what is going on. You might just as well try a baby in arms." This "baby" was thereupon commit-

[30] *Ottawa Citizen*, May 18, 1968.
[31] G. D. Roberts, *Law and Life*, W. H. Allen Ltd., London, 1964.
[32] He was condemned to death at his second trial, but reprieved by the Home Secretary.

ted to an institution from which he promptly made his escape; and before he could be retaken, strangled his third victim. This time apparently there was at least no hesitation about trying "a baby in arms."

The presiding judge at the second trial put two questions to the defense psychologist. "Do you think he had the design to kill?" Answer—"His desire to kill seems to me to spring from his desire to pay back the police because of his hatred of them. Whether that was his only motive, I cannot say." Question—"If that is so, had he the intelligence not to select a policeman to strangle, but a defenceless little girl?" Answer—"Evidently, my Lord."

Roberts, who was one of the prosecutors of Nazi war criminals at Nuremberg, and who undoubtedly had his fill of human beastliness, must have known what he was talking about when he commented, "Streffen was driven by some sadistic instinct, craving power and domination, and deriving satisfaction from choking these little children, and watching their death struggles. There is unfortunately no limit to the cruelties perpetrated on fellow humans." Commenting further on the absurdities into which courts and juries have fallen in permitting the plea of insanity in too many instances, he observes tersely that "despite what murderers say in the witness box, they usually know full well what they are doing at the time of the crime. They deserve to hang."

Testifying in the famous Durham case, a psychiatrist has epitomized this so-called sickness in terms that are far from sympathetic: "The symptoms ordinarily associated with psychopathic personalities are irrational thinking, general unreliability, untruthfulness, insincerity, and lack of shame. Such patients usually exhibit poor judgment, although they have superficial charm and intelligence. They tend to engage in fantastic and uninviting behavior which may or may not be induced by alcohol. Their interpersonal relations are poor. They do things to get their own ends and show little concern for the effect it may have on others. These people are frequently liars and their demands on others are usually excessive."[33]

Now it should be settled that no semantic difficulty will be resolved by attributing to such creatures "a high degree of fragmentation." Their "diminished capacity" is never such that they are unable to denounce the misconduct of persons other than themselves. Whether demented or not, they may still contain within themselves a cluster of characteristics common to the more animal-like members of the human race. One can be both insane and malignant, even as one can be both insane and gentle. The fact that such an aggressor may be afflicted either mentally or physically will not in most cases rob him of this awareness. Like King Henry VIII of England, he might have been tormented by syphilis for the greater part of his life; or like the bloodthirsty Marat, might have contracted a loathsome skin disease while hiding in a sewer from the royalist police. He might, like the Tsar Ivan IV, have lived in daily terror of his unruly nobles throughout his entire childhood. Afflictions and perils such as these, certainly in the case of ordinary people, are a claim upon the world's commiseration. But when are we to start feeling sorry for them? Only when they begin venting their pent-up rage on others?

We are brought face to face with a basic question. On what grounds do we exonerate an offender who is insane, even though such insanity is complete and beyond all doubt? On a hardheaded view of the matter, and basing ourselves solely on the premise that the safety of the public is all that matters, there can be no good reason for treating an offender more leniently merely because he is insane. He is far more of a burden than one who is sane; and the possibility of rehabilitation is exceedingly remote. The German Nazis had an answer. They liquidated the insane, criminals and noncriminals alike. They acted in accordance with a kind of monstrous logic; but it was a logic that no civilized society would endure. In the

[33]Simon, *op. cit.*, p. 42.

civilized world, logic is tempered with mercy. It is pity for the fallen condition of a fellow mortal that forbids a decently ordered community to punish one of its members whenever it is clear that he really meant no harm.

IRRESISTIBLE IMPULSE

That one's reason need not be altogether dethroned in order that he might be absolved from responsibility has long been acknowledged. In particular instances, capacity to distinguish between right and wrong could fail, even without a clouding of the entire consciousness. As already mentioned, even this doctrine has been held to be too limited, as not affording those of borderline intellect sufficient scope for exoneration. The extremist critics of the test of moral responsibility, confident in their knowledge of the internal fabric of the human mind, have rallied around the doctrine of irresistible impulse as the ultimate in scientific sophistication.

Now it requires no great discernment to discover that this quixotic philosophy is nothing but an extension of the liberal and laissez-faire attitude towards all crime in general. The supposed disparity between legal and medical insanity has been so far cancelled out by some court decisions that what has been ruled as being temporary insanity in the legal sense, corresponds very closely to a condition to which, it is claimed, any normal person could be prone. The noted anticapitalpunishmentarian Clarence Darrow is reputed to have written, "All persons are potential murderers, needing only time and circumstance." This is about as sapient a bit of philosophy as declaring that all persons are potential winners of $100,000 at the Irish Sweepstakes, needing only time and circumstance. The possibility remains an overwhelming one notwithstanding: few persons are destined to become either murderers or winners of the Irish Sweepstakes. What they are under certain circumstances capable of doing or becoming has no relevance to what they actually are or actually do.

Juries without number have in recent years allowed glib

defense attorneys to persuade them that persons ordinarily in full possession of their faculties had committed horrendous deeds through their being impelled by an adamantine thrust. "Samuel Leibowitz convinced not one but a dozen juries that those who killed while in the grip of some mental disorder were not guilty because the blow was struck, the knife was plunged, the gun was fired by 'the hand of God.' "[34]

Endless vistas are opened up by the introduction of this newfangled theology into matters judicial, and not alone in cases of killing. A motorist charged with reckless driving might well contend that it was really the hand of God that turned his wheel too far to the left, or that poured those few extra ounces into his glass. Further than that, it could be suggested that his transference of blame to the Deity could, on being extended to commercial dealings, lead to some truly remarkable conclusions. The civil law too, be it recalled, provides relief in certain cases of mental lapse. Under the civil law, a contract can be voided where it is proven that one of the parties was pushed into it by some overpowering momentum. If the definition of insanity is now to include one whom God has capriciously deprived of his will power, if only temporarily, why not likewise in commercial dealings, more especially in matters that have turned out unfortunately for one of the contracting parties? Such a party has purchased through a broker or promoter some oil stocks, a purchase he later regretted. He is entitled to have his money refunded since he is able to prove that on the day he placed his order his mind had been clouded by some great tragedy, such as the sudden demise of his mother-in-law, and was during that entire day in a state bordering on coma. The check that he ought not to have written on that particular day, was written "by the hand of God."

All penalties for iniquities rest upon the concept of freedom of will, which, it has been alleged, the social sciences have shown to be nonexistent. Vengeance and punishment are thus unjust and uncalled for, since the behavior of all men derives

[34]Quentin Reynolds, *Courtroom*, Popular Library, Toronto, p. 151.

from impulses that are predetermined and irresistible. Let us consider the meaning of "irresistible impulse" by asking, first of all, when is an impulse resistible. It deserves to be stated, by way of a preliminary, that of any impulse that proves resistible, so that it engenders no overt act, little or nothing can be known. It remains locked and out of sight within the recesses of the mind.

That impulses of every kind enter unbidden into the consciousness of us all is a matter of everyday experience. To obey them or not to obey them surely becomes a matter of choice or decision on our part. These impulses, even when unresisted, can be good as well as bad, constructive and destructive. Thus, I may have at 1:00 in the afternoon an urge to enter a restaurant, not having eaten since 8:00. My impulse is not only irresistible, but rational likewise. However, at about 2:30 in the afternoon of the same day, I am beset by another impulse to eat again. But my inner voice reminds me that I have eaten not so long ago. If, notwithstanding, I still persist in entering that eating place, my impulse once again proves itself to be irresistible, though not as salutary.

Now it ought to be fairly obvious that one who kills or maims while totally and incontestably the madman, as envisaged in the days of Chief Justice Sir Matthew Hale, can only be doing so as a result of that very irresistible impulse postulated by these modernist authorities in human behavior. Any other interpretation could only be self-contradictory. Acts of this nature are of course excusable, and have been so for centuries. Less excusable, even in the eyes of these radical behaviorists, it must be assumed, is it when there is an awareness of the wickedness of the projected deed; but it is performed, nevertheless, as a result of what they are pleased to denominate an irresistible impulse. In such instances, the viable moral perception of the doer could be expected to act as some sort of brake on this impulse; but we are assured that it need not be so. The impulse to act in berserk fashion may here too prove irresistible, as in the first example mentioned.

Now to the psychiatric theory of insanity, propounded as a

more liberal and modern approach to the problem, a number of objections here present themselves. To begin with, to show the same indulgence to a malefactor who knows what he is doing as to one who does not, is a doctrine altogether too preposterous to swallow. But further. There also arises the question as to the why and wherefore of the supposedly inexorable nemesis that has presided over the offense in question.

The "irresistible impulse" to do something bad may on occasion stem from a provocative act on the part of the victim. This might induce a mental or emotional blowup that, far from being a manifestation of insanity, could be looked upon as quite normal and predictable under the circumstances. Some great wrong, or insult, or injustice, might bring about an act of retaliation, which, even if not completely justifiable, could be excusable at least to some extent. "Surely oppression maketh a wise man mad" (Ecclesiastes 7:7). But there are impulses of another kind, equally irresistible, no doubt, which to society may be less worthy of toleration, even though they too may be condoned by many lawyers turned psychiatrists. Such impulses may have their source in a vortex of anger, hatred, or jealousy; or in some overweening lust for other people's possessions. Hence, the question of moral responsibility for crimes committed, cast out of doors by emancipated thinkers, is here to be seen as making a re-entry through some other door. The theory of irresistible impulse, even if accepted, is neither a contradiction nor an infringement of the traditional doctrine of moral responsibility.

If we are to accept the thesis that intention, as a criterion, is to be replaced by some other directive, why not do so for all wrongdoers, sane or insane, and treat all without distinction as acting under an ungovernable mechanical drive? The bank robber, whose mental soundness is not questioned, could be allowed to plead, nevertheless, that he became that way as a result of an inevitable chain of circumstances, beginning with an unfortunate childhood. To have been tossed about helplessly by bad home environment, by lack of employment, lack of education and training, or by discrimination is certainly excuse for wrongdoing at least as valid as having been born with a low intelligence. As questions of fact they are certainly far easier to verify than the prevalence of some nebulous state of mind.

That all human beings, when they perform their actions, in effect act under impulses that could be termed irresistible is, from the standpoint of criminal administration, a discovery of no great significance. Ambition, avarice, hunger, love, self-love, vanity, friendship, generosity, public spirit, revenge, hatred—all these passions, mixed in various degree and distributed throughout society, have been from the beginning of the world and unto this very day the source of all actions and enterprises. Each and every one of the impulses resulting from these passions will unavoidably be weighed on the scale of ethics and entail an imputation of responsibility to the doer.

It may well be, as Germany's greatest poet and philosopher Goethe once wrote, "By eternal laws of iron ruled must all fulfill the cycle of their destiny." All human actions, for good and evil, are said by some thinkers, ancient and modern, to be predestined and hence fatalistically ordained. It does not really matter whether you believe this or not. But if you do believe it, you must do so with logical consistency. You must believe that in the same way as men's actions are subject to an uncontrollable necessity, so too must be the thoughts and feelings engendered by these actions. When the friendly jailor, handing the lethal cup to Socrates, bade him drink "because it must needs be so," he was in effect telling the condemned man that the cycle of his destiny had been inexorably circuited by the thoughts and sentiments aroused towards him of his judges and fellow citizens.

When a man shoots or stabs or places a bomb or sets fire to a building or commits a rape or a kidnapping, he is perhaps acting under the spell of the law of causation, most of whose links are invisible but nonetheless present. But the public and private indignation that this act brings out must then be seen as an extension of the same unbreakable chain, and as no less dictated and predestined. Further extensions of this chain of cause and effect would be his apprehension, his conviction, and his ultimate liberation through the interventions of some do-gooders. The discovery by numerous psychiatrists and lawyers that men, criminal or law-abiding, have no freedom to choose, is a thesis which you are at liberty either to accept or to reject. Paradoxically, this controversial discovery, and the varied reception given to it, is the best evidence of all that human beings really do enjoy a freedom to choose.

CHAPTER 7

Conclusions

IN THE CLASH OF PERSPECTIVES OVER CAPITAL PUNISHment, the question as to which side commands a majority is important. A recent poll indicates that 48 percent of the population of the United States favor the retention of the death penalty, 38 percent are opposed, while 14 percent are undecided.[1] In both Canada and Great Britain, a similar preponderance of sentiment is known to exist. And yet in all three countries, it is the minority view that presently has the predominant voice. Such consistent failure on the part of the majority to assert itself calls for an explanation.

In any free society, electoral offices are filled demonstrably according to majority vote: and from this principle there is hardly ever any deviation. It also goes without saying that all legislative enactments are adopted in accordance with this pattern. Likewise by vote of the majority are all decisions handed down by courts of higher instance. In all these matters, the democratic principle of majority rule is held unswervingly. Nevertheless, this tenet, firmly rooted though it may appear, hardly penetrates very much further, or else does so only haltingly.

The Founding Fathers of the United States, though in theory

[1] *Time*, June 6, 1969, p. 29.

committed to majority rule, had certain misgivings about the excesses that unrestricted sway of the majority could entail. In fact, the first ten amendments to the Constitution, passed early in the nineteenth century, were meant to neutralize this possibility. An observer of the infant Republic, the Frenchman Alexis de Tocqueville, in his pioneer treatise *Democracy in America,* had a note of caution as to an emerging tyranny of the majority. A later reviewer, Lord Bryce, in his classic *The American Commonwealth,* expressed a similar concern. Even the English prophet of democracy, John Stuart Mill, was himself apprehensive of the hazards lurking in majority rule; and in his famous *Essay on Liberty* spoke out against "a government of privilege in favour of the numerical majority." None of these doubters thought of the possibility of a democracy being hobbled by what might well be referred to as "the tyranny of the minority."

The size and populousness of modern states are such that the individual member regards himself as nothing but an insignificant cog. Accordingly, his response to matters of public interest is apt to be either dull or cynical. Being at a loss as to how to coalesce with others of like mind, he too readily abandons the field of controversy to those who are not apathetic, and to those who refuse to surrender to the belief that the individual by himself can do nothing. Hence it becomes altogether normal for the silent majority merely to look on as things happen around them.

In the affairs of the world, a relatively small minority can be more assertive than a passive majority. In war, this has many times been proven, and in the internal upheavals of nations likewise. All the major revolutions, such as the French Jacobin, the Russian Bolshevik, and the German Nazi, were minority enterprises. The war of the American Revolution was activated by not more than a third of the inhabitants of the American colonies. Time and again has it happened that in war and other armed struggles, minorities have prevailed over majorities. What has often been the case in war, has been hardly less so in times of peace. Augment this observation with the corollary that it is not in the nature of minorities to be respectful of the wishes of the majority, even among political sects supposedly dedicated to the principles of democracy.

There happens to be a deep-seated psychological basis for the repeated defeats of majority opinion within democratic societies. It is a fashionable assumption that in all matters of controversy extremists and fanatics are equally to be found on both sides. But this simplified habit of looking at things, I consider to be at odds with the true situation. For example, an altogether too familiar usage of language impels us to divide the attitudes of the population into "right" and "left." Actually, rightists and leftists are not opposites at all. They are more like next-door neighbors. No matter what the issue, be it racial, social, religious, or whatnot, you will discover some far-out apostles, call them leftists or rightists or by some other name. Invariably, however—and this is the point of my argument—you will find that the extremists and activists, no matter how designated, are more heavily engaged on one side of the issue than on the other.

The side that is the more heavily weighted with passion, be it a majority or a minority, is almost certain to gain the upper hand, for the time being at least. Militancy has its undeniable advantages. Where it exists, there, likewise, will you find determination, discipline, self-assurance, and organization. At the same time, among those who are on the defending side you will quite often discover little of these virile qualities. Not being rabid in their views, they have correspondingly less energy, will power, and keenness for the struggle.

In common with all contentious issues, the same holds good as regards the debate on capital punishment. Here too, absolutism is found to be entirely on one side. On the side of the abolitionists, we do indeed find moderates as well as extremists. Extremists in behalf of abolition were the men and women, in the days when executions were still being carried out, who would rise up early in the morning, beset the jails, and scream their disapproval. They were the people who raised a mighty clamor on hearing of a projected execution in some part of the free world, without caring very much whether the condemned was innocent or guilty. Extremists were those who would have spared the life of an Eichmann, or who, like the immoderate Clarence Darrow, maintained that the state in hanging a convicted killer was guilty of an even greater crime than that of the one who was hanged.

On the other side of the debate, among those who still favor the death penalty, you will discover no parallel depth of feeling. You are not likely to find anyone who would start a parade and create an uproar in favor of the gallows as a means of restoring law and order. No one, no matter how strongly in favor, would approve making a public spectacle out of a hanging, or take pleasure in witnessing such a performance. Nor would anyone nowadays advocate, as did Chief Justice Lord Ellenborough in 1810, that for a theft of more than five shillings worth the penalty of death should be continued. It is even doubtful if you could find anyone on this continent or in Great Britain who would insist on hanging for all murderers without any exception.

CAPITAL AND OTHER PUNISHMENT

The whole question of liquidating murderers must be viewed within the framework of a pluralist society, a society in which divergent opinions must all be given at least some heed. We carry on our lives within a free society in which conflicting viewpoints of both majorities and minorities deserve respect and attention. The majority ought not to dismiss out of hand the wishes of the minority, nor on the other hand should a minority be permitted to assume the prerogatives of the majority. Under a system of give and take, it is altogether possible for the death penalty to be retained and abolished at the same time.

In the days when hanging or the electric chair was the automatic end for all persons convicted of first degree murder, many such lives might well have been spared by reason of alleviating factors, even though guilt was unquestionable.

"Murder to the average well adjusted man is a repugnant, unnatural act. And yet each year hundreds of average men whose minds have temporarily veered from the norm find themselves accused of first degree murder. There are many reasons why an ordinarily law-abiding and decent citizen will suddenly commit an act of violence, an act which has no relationship to his normal intent and which is a negation of every decent impulse and instinct in his character."[2] This is indisputable. Of such episodes explainable by "an overwhelming pressure of anguish," examples are to be found in Reynold's account of the exploits of Samuel J. Leibowitz, the noted criminal lawyer. He was able to secure the release of a woman who in order to defend herself shot a bestial Nazi; likewise, of an elderly husband married to a women younger than himself, who kept on taunting him by telling him of her infidelities; of an outraged husband who shot a man, supposedly a friend and a frequent guest at his home, on discovering that he had been carrying on an intrigue with his wife. These, as well as numerous other instances, such as are frequently reported in the press as well as in professional literature, are all deserving of clemency. In some instances, the provocation has been of such an extreme nature as to exonerate the killer totally, while in others, a measure of culpability remains, but certainly not of a degree deserving of extreme penalization.

There are very often grounds for leniency, though not necessarily those put forward by the chorus of sentimentalists. On the wrong side of toleration is the youth of the prisoner or the fact that the killer is female. Neither poverty nor wealth, neither being of a good family nor being of a poor one is of itself a good basis for reprieve. Generalized guidelines, such as the distinction between capital and noncapital murder, are not entitled to much respect. As often as not the noncapital murderer is more wicked than the representative of the other variety. Poisoning is not reckoned as capital; and yet it is invariably premeditated and accompanied by the most intense

[2]Quentin Reynolds, *Courtroom.*

suffering on the part of the victim. A prime factor to be considered is the manner in which the life has been taken, and the amount of torment that was incidental. Where there has been a display of sadism, there ought to be no occasion for sparing the life of the murderer.

It should be a cause for wonderment that the taking of two or more lives is not in our society considered a more heinous crime than the taking of only one. Where there is some ground for mercy in the case of a single life being taken, there ought to be none whatever in cases of multiple killing.

A highly relevant factor is the character of the victim. He might have been a person that the world could well do without. Oswald assassinated President Kennedy; and Oswald in turn was gunned down by Jack Ruby. In a technical sense, Ruby in killing Oswald committed exactly the same offense as did Oswald in shooting the President. Morally, there was a world of difference. Ruby, had he not died of an illness, would have been deserving of some punishment for having taken the law into his own hands, and for nothing more.

I would suggest that the sentence of death be imposed only in comparatively rare instances; but that it need not be restricted to cases of murder. A distinguished jurist of the nineteenth century made a just observation: "I think that political offences should in some cases be punished with death. People should be made to understand that to attack the existing state of society is equivalent to risking their own lives."[3] The numerous bigoted and inhuman exaggerations once given to the law of treason have fortunately long been defunct. And yet the fundamental essence of this crime must still be underlined. Treason and conspiracy in our own time are no more out of fashion than is murder or any other major villainy. Consideration ought to be given to imposing the death penalty, even in peacetime, on those guilty of endangering their country by handing over military or other secrets to a potential enemy.

Assassination of men holding any kind of public office, in-

[3]Sir James Stephen, *A History of the Criminal Law of England*, vol. 1, p. 478.

cluding policemen, of course, should be regarded as both treason and murder; and ought under no circumstances to be treated with any leniency. The lives of men who devote themselves to the service of the state or community suffer from an undue exposure: and it should follow that the state in its turn owes them a double measure of protection. Attempts on the lives of men holding public office would become far less frequent were it generally known that even a bare attempt would be treated as a capital crime. Equally to be so treated should be the placing or throwing of a bomb in all instances that result in injury to persons. Such acts are inordinately malicious.

Offenses against property alone are not in civilized countries punishable by death, and ought never to be so. However, the surrealist notion that life may in no circumstances whatever be taken in defense of property is another matter. Opposition to the shooting down of rioters engaged in looting and burning has been voiced by politicians on the maxim that "life is more important than property." Situations could arise, however, when life is not more important than property. If my building is about to be destroyed or my shop about to be looted, I could be forgiven for thinking that what I have saved and accumulated in the course of a lifetime ought to be defended most strenuously, even if in so doing the life of a bandit should be imperilled. Failure to protect the property of any honest citizen by as much force as may be needed because of a misplaced reverence for the life of some worthless desperado can only encourage the boldness and criminality of society's baser elements.

Crimes against property, when unchecked, escalate, as time goes on, into crimes against the person. For preventing bloodshed and violence, measures other than the death penalty suggest themselves. If instead of a mere fine of twenty-five dollars the punishment for carrying an unregistered weapon were really substantial, fewer pockets would have guns nestling inside them. Also, it is mathematically certain that the longer a gunman is kept behind bars, the less time will be left to him for shooting at anyone. A reversal of the present indulgence towards all manner of thievery and other offenses would of itself have a pacifying effect. Codified sentences for various offenses already mild enough by the standards of earlier times have by custom of the courts been reduced even further. But this is not all. Through the intervention of parole boards, even the diminished sentences of the courts are subject to still further attrition. An observation of Beccaria throws a strong light on this matter.

> In proportion as punishments become milder, the need for clemency and pardon becomes less. . . . This will seem a hard truth to anyone who lives amid the disorder of a penal system in which pardon and mercy are necessarily proportionate to the absurdity of the laws, and the appalling severity of the sentences. . . . But let it be considered that . . . showing men that crime may be pardoned or that punishment is not their inevitable consequence encourages the hope of impunity. . . . So let the laws be inexorable and also those who administer them in particular cases; but let the lawmaker be gentle, lenient, and humane.[4]

CORPORAL PUNISHMENT

Under the criminal code of Canada, whipping can be made part of the punishment for rape and attempted rape, armed robbery, choking and drugging, indecent assault, incest, and sexual intercourse with a girl under fourteen. The retention of this sanction will inevitably be bound up in the long run with that of capital punishment. Those advocating the extreme penalty cannot in all logic but approve of one that is less severe. Those, on the other hand, who are opposed to the taking of life under any circumstances, will easily enough discover reasons for opposing as well any form of physical punishment.

This is not an agreeable topic; but neither is the situation that must bring it to the fore. Is the resort to a controlled and regulated violence by those in authority a proper answer to the unbridled violence of the criminal element? Answers in both

[4]As quoted by Alessandro Manzoni, *The Column of Infamy,* p. 58.

the affirmative and the negative are to be expected. No less divided on this question are members of the judiciary, as they are on all other controversial matters connected with criminal law administration.

A magistrate in the city of Toronto has been quoted as saying, "When I originally came to the bench eleven years ago, I thought that there was a place for the lash; but when I talked to my wife and daughters about it, they told me that if I ever passed that kind of sentence on anyone, there was no point in my coming home." One of his colleagues, apparently less subject to guidance by his wife and daughters, announced during the same interview that his earlier belief in the old-fashioned corrective was still undiminished.[5]

A definite stand on this question was taken only a short time ago in a report to the Canadian government by the Ouimet Commission. This committee found that "the present laws permitting corporal punishment of offenders are an astonishing anachronism and should be repealed."[6] The list of "anachronisms" in the existing laws as laid bare by this body of bleeding hearts seems to have been extensive indeed. Among its one hundred and eighteen specific recommendations are included proposals for "less use of the power of arrest," "judicial ability to discharge an offender without sentence," "detaining people before trial as seldom as possible," "automatic annulments of most criminal records," and "the establishment of hostel-type detention centres instead of jails." These, along with the other accommodating proposals of these foolhardy men, were they to be adopted, might constitute a veritable Magna Carta for our country's criminal population. All this at a time when, in the words of the prophet Ezekiel, "the land is full of bloody crimes, and the city is full of violence" (9:9).

Within the expurgated society postulated by these utopian reformers, the one and only response to insolence and disorder, whether in the home, in the school, in the university, or in the state, is the very gentlest of prodding along the road of

[5] *Montreal Star*, July 10, 1969.
[6] *Montreal Star*, September 25, 1969.

repentance of all sinners, no matter how vicious and intractable they may be. In the city of Montreal, known as the crime capital of Canada, if not North America, there are magistrates who, in pronouncing sentences, inform the prisoners, almost as a matter of protocol, that they are "lucky" their sentences do not include the physical chastisement that their misdeeds would have warranted. Such fatherly admonitions are intended hopefully to instill a mood of contrition in the breasts of the fortunate detainees. At times, indeed, these same magistrates, when in a really severe mood, have been known to administer what in journalistic parlance is known as "a tongue lashing," a substitute, apparently, for the more palpable variety discountenanced nowadays by all good people as only "adding to the brutality of society."

What has indeed added greatly to the brutality of society, or more accurately, to the brutality to which society has been exposed, has been the rejection of corporal punishment in the name of a presumptive higher civilization. Despite the aversion of oversensitive persons, corporal punishment enjoys a number of singular advantages. Its severity could be easily regulated, making it highly conformable to many offenses, ranging from insubordination in the schools to assaults in the streets. In cases of youthful rowdyism, it could be an excellent substitute for a fine or imprisonment. Even for more serious offenses, its application could serve to cut down all terms of imprisonment and thereby answer some of the objections that have been made as to the deleterious effects of prison life, to say nothing of the overcrowded conditions of the prisons.

THE WORSHIP OF YOUTH

The slackening of discipline that characterizes contemporary society is intimately tied to an unseasonable concern for "the cravings of the youth" and their precocious opinions. To these pampered and inviolable "kids" must be attributed much of the surcharge of criminality by which the cities of this continent have been scarred. With all their turbulence and "dissent," these juveniles and near juveniles are easily manipulated by those having an interest in directing them—with the exception of their parents, of course. Among the anomalies of our enlightened age, is the failure of politicians and educators alike to recognize that teenagers, as well as many university students, are only one stage removed from the intellectual level of school children. Developed physically and sexually they may be, but certainly not mentally and emotionally. It should by this time be abundantly clear that these shaggy "freshmen" and "sophomores" are not nearly as grown up as their growth of hair might indicate.

The early Romans, wise in their understanding of the facts of life, refused to consider mere puberty an insignia of maturity. Between childhood and manhood, they acknowledged an intermediate stage, that of the *adolescentes.* Only those who had attained the age of twenty-five were qualified to wear the *toga virilis* and to participate as equals in the affairs of the state.

ORDER AND THE COURTS

The deficiencies of criminal procedure become even more glaring when it comes to dealing with members of powerful crime syndicates and key figures in revolutionary enterprises. In the case of such individuals and organizations, successful prosecution can be balked at every stage, beginning with their arrest by the police and ending with their final appeals before the highest courts. As regards the Mafia, it is presently admitted that there is no effective means for fighting it "that would not put civil liberties in jeopardy." Staggering in this connection was the confession of the late Senator Robert Kennedy: "No one has yet resolved the puzzle of working out the constitutional problem."[7] So insuperable are these constitutional roadblocks that the tendency has been to abandon criminal prosecutions in favor of law suits before the civil courts, where

[7]Article by Max Lerner, *Montreal Gazette,* August 5, 1969.

the obstacles in the way of some kind of penalization are deemed less formidable.[8]

For a depressing account of the impossible obstacles to such criminal prosecutions presented by the existing rules of evidence and the formalities of trial by jury, the reader is referred to a twenty-six-page report contained in a special supplement of *Life* magazine on a recent trial conducted against four prominent members of the Mafia.[9] Out of a host of revealing passages, I shall confine myself to quoting but one:

> Over and over as the jurors are selected, the judge has warned them to avoid outside knowledge of the case; to read nothing, listen to nothing, talk to no one, seek no knowledge, accept no knowledge. They will be men groping in the dark. The trial will be a process not of discovery and enlightenment but of deception and concealment. Of the 30 or so people directly involved in the trial, the twelve men with the greatest responsibility—the jurors—will end up knowing the least about the case. Since the law requires that the criminal background of the defendants be kept from jurors, the defense lawyers are free to castigate the prosecution's witnesses as bank robbers; but the prosecutor will never be allowed to retaliate by pointing out that the man who masterminded the robberies so referred to is the principal defendant.

It should be conceded that the war against the crime syndicate is hampered by weaknesses that go beyond the illogical rules of method. A valiant attempt before the Italian courts to destroy the Sicilian Mafia ended recently in a like failure, when it was declared that the evidence gathered against the seventeen defendants was "insufficient" as regards each and every one of them. Fully five years had been devoted by the Italian prosecuting attorneys, assisted by United States agents, in preparing the case against these men, all of whom were known underworld characters and who would have been incapable of giving satisfactory and believable accounts of their day-to-day

[8] *Time*, May 2, 1969.
[9] James Mills, "The People *vs.* Sonny Franzese and Others," *Life*, August 30, 1968.

activities. The evidence thus laboriously accumulated, and then rejected by the officiating judge, was contained in twenty-five volumes.[10]

Justice is hardly less impotent when it comes to dealing with Soviet agents and their North American helpers. In 1950, Congress passed the McCarran Anti-Subversive Law, which required the registration of all organizations dominated by a foreign power. To date, neither the Communist party nor any one of its fronts has been obliged to comply with this law, thanks to the protection afforded by the courts.

Antisedition laws of state legislatures have been held unconstitutional. Loyalty oaths required of students seeking government loans have been outlawed; university professors refusing to testify about subversive activities before legislative committees have been upheld in their refusal.[11]

In Canada, there have been of late at least two instances in which governmental employees were found to be betraying their country. In the first instance, prosecution was waived on the well-grounded fear that under the niceties of conventional procedure, a trial "would blow the cover off two or three agents who are performing a very valuable function." In the more recent scandal, the exposed employee, whose name has not been divulged, was told to "resign or face unpleasant consequences." He took the advice, and has since disappeared, taking with him secrets of which nothing is known.[12] The reason given in this instance for not prosecuting, as in the earlier, was that prosecution could not be instituted without unmasking the antiespionage efforts of the Royal Canadian Mounted Police. Also, government antiespionage agents are said to have been cautioned against "the kind of entrapment that could be declared illegal by the courts." Taking all these hindrances into account, one cannot avoid harboring the impression that in cases of serious insurrection, be they nationwide or local, the amount of assistance from the courts that the authorities could

[10] *Montreal Star*, July 5, 1968.
[11] *Sweezy* v. *New Hampshire*, 354 U.S. 234; *Uphaus* v. *Wyman*, 360 U.S. 72; *U.S.A.* v. *Barenblatt*, 350 U.S. 1081.
[12] *Montreal Star*, September 25, 1968.

look for would be minimal indeed. This matter calls for some further elaboration.

Government, we have been taught to believe, is made up of three distinct parts, the legislative, the executive, and the judicial. Concerning this trinitarian concept, some reservation should be made, however. In Russia, and generally throughout the nonfree world, the judiciary undoubtedly serves as an arm of government. In the free world, to the contrary, the judiciary is so far emancipated from control by either the legislature or the executive that we can say it exists as something entirely apart from government.

To be sure, judges owe their appointments to cabinets of the various levels, and they are paid out of the public treasury. Once appointed, however, they are subject to virtually no control. Except only in cases of gross misfeasance, their performance in office is subject to no scrutiny. Unlike business executives, members of the professions and civil servants, they are made to suffer no inconvenience as a result of incompetent rulings. Neither their personal eccentricities nor their overstepping of the limits of discretion is made subject to overt criticism. Also, knowing themselves to be free of lay control, they are on occasion tempted to determine matters coming before them not according to the law as it is written, but according to what in their opinion the law ought to be.

Now all this autonomy has its advantages and disadvantages. Under the constitutional theory of separation of powers, an independent judiciary is intended above all to safeguard the private citizen from the high-handed attentions of public officials. Undeniably this purpose has been achieved, and no one will deny that this has been all to the good. Some negative feature must be taken into account nevertheless.

In clashes between constituted authority on the one hand and its numerous and assorted enemies on the other, now occurring with increasing frequency, the position of the judiciary is, in theory at least, that of an umpire. In practice, members of the judiciary are known to lean either on the side of the government or on the side of its opponents. A large body of citizens at the present time is prone to regard all resistance to government in a somewhat benevolent light, and as heralding a better order of things. It should not be surprising, accordingly, that there are members of the bench who partake of this line of thought. Also, members of the judiciary are by and large recruited from among the ranks of lawyers practicing criminal law, who are by habit of thought defense-oriented. Some reflection of this thinking manifests itself almost daily. After a night of rioting and looting in the city of Montreal recently, one magistrate distinguished himself by handing down a series of condemnations of one-day imprisonments plus fines of $25.00 to those having the good fortune to be brought before him.

The handing down of such rosewater sentences does nothing to shield society from its enemies; and yet no direct remedy is to be found. Involved here are questions of human nature as well as ideological attitudes about which, in the absence of a sudden change in the public's conscience, nothing can be done. A purge of the judiciary is of course out of the question. Not all judges can be regarded as being soft on criminals. In any event, who could really decide as to who are the soft ones and who are not the soft ones, and where would be the line of differentiation? The problem can only be approached from some other direction.

SPECIAL TRIBUNALS

The eighteenth-century poet Jonathan Swift suggested that laws are like cobwebs. The small and feeble are caught, but the wasps and hornets break through. If we go back far enough into the past, to a time when there was hardly any law, even the wasps and hornets were never really safe. There have been occasions without number, when neither wealth nor position conferred sustained safety. If anything, the richer you were, and therefore the more conspicuous, the greater your exposure. A change of fortune was nearly always lurking around some corner to catapult into disaster some powerful minister, or popular hero, or opulent banker. It was quite routine, in Asia especially, for a ruler with only a word or wave of the hand to end the life of a magnate who incurred his displeasure and whom he came to regard as dangerous.

In England, in the course of time, and with the growing prestige of the law, such lightning procedures came to be less and less acceptable. In the case of obscure malefactors the Common Law magistracy could be depended upon to mete out stern enough justice. But there were dilemmas in cases where the suspects were wealthy and influential landowners. To summon such a culprit before a judge and jury of his peers, while at the same time a plentiful array of his retainers would be lounging in and around the courthouse, must have been for the prosecutor and his witnesses a chilling experience. For persons of this category, whenever seized in the midst of plots, factions and intrigues, there had to be devised a swifter and surer method for bringing to heel than that afforded by the wavering Common Law courts.

In the year 1571, a plot against Queen Elizabeth I, which could have plunged England into a religious war similar to those then raging on the Continent, was narrowly defeated by the timely arrests of the Dukes of Norfolk and Northumberland. The complicity of these nobles was beyond question. The problem, however, was how to dispose of such powerful men otherwise than by bringing them before a court of assizes with its cumbersome and dilatory process. A method was indeed at hand. The evidence against these ringleaders was submitted to the houses of Parliament, called into session as a trial court. Without any needless fuss or delay they were condemned to death by what was then known as a "bill of attainder."

Some decades later, Parliament, facing another crisis, acted in the same expeditious manner by destroying its own particular enemy, the able and ambitious minister of King Charles I, the Earl of Strafford, when it was revealed that he was planning to bring into England an army from Ireland in order to overawe the parliamentary opposition. Throughout the centuries and in diverse parts there have been numerous instances of assemblies that were primarily legislative taking unto themselves judicial functions as well. The Roman Senate often sat as a court, passing sentence on aspiring revolutionists such as Gracchus, and conspirators like Catalina and Sejanus.

The clothing of lawmaking bodies with direct judicial functions of course had its sinister aspect. More often than not, it was a shrouding of base political motives and a means of prostituting justice. Also, in line with the streamlined method of bypassing the regular courts were the operations of the dreaded Court of Star Chamber of the Tudor and Stuart monarchs, of which court a vivid recollection remained long after its suppression. It was their recoil from this engine of oppression that caused the framers of the American Constitution to write into its very first article a prohibition of all retroactive legislation, including, of course, legislation directed expressly against named individuals. But a form of legislation that to statesmen of a past century seemed outrageous, need not be so regarded for all time thereafter. On at least one occasion within recent memory, such tying of the hands of a nation's elected representatives was proven to be unfortunate, as will now be related.

During the Second World War, the activities and political sympathies of three United States civil servants were looked into by the House Committee on Un-American Activities and by the Federal Bureau of Investigation. It was found that they had all the time been outspoken Nazi sympathizers. Subsequently, the reports of these two agencies were considered by the House Appropriations Committee, with the result that an Urgent Deficiency Appropriation Act of 1943 contained a provision that no salary be paid to these disloyal public servants. On appeal to the Supreme Court, this punitive act was declared to be a bill of attainder and hence unconstitutional.[13] The three Nazi traitors collected their salaries, along with all the others.

Who at the present time are the wasps and hornets whom

[13] *United States* v. *Lovett*, 328 U.S. 303 (1946).

the law's cobwebs are unable to contain? They are not any longer dukes and other adventurous nobles bent on subverting monarchies, and engaging in dynastic and religious quarrels. The hornets of our time, who escape so easily, are the sellers of military secrets to a potential enemy whom the Canadian or American government finds it unwise to prosecute. Others are Fasco-Communist terrorists in the Province of Quebec who are released on light bail and permitted in the meanwhile to carry on their activities. Or Black Panthers in the U.S.A. Still others are members of the Mafia whom the law enforcement authorities can only harass in some small way by proceedings against them before the civil courts. The authorities who are nowadays on the defensive against such elements are no longer tyrannical and absolutist royal dynasties, but rather the freely chosen representatives of the people.

No doubt, the extraordinary measures that I now propose will be greeted with the usual cries of "witch-hunting," "overreacting," "fascism," "police state," and similar epithets. It is time, however, for the public to start fearing real things rather than mere words. With the crime situation continuing to worsen, with the apostles of anarchy growing ever more assertive, would it be better that private citizens continue to arm themselves as they have for some time been doing; and perhaps be tempted to take matters into their own hands sooner or later?

An effective and orderly method for democratic governments to sterilize all public enemies, political and nonpolitical alike, would be the return, during temporary periods, to the ancient system of combining legislative and judicial functions. Such legislative tribunals would make no pretense whatever of being neutral as between the authorities on the one hand and the antisocial elements on the other. They would care nothing about intricate procedures, but everything about fact-finding. Subject to their attention would not be the humble and the poor and the wretched; but only the strong and the dangerous —the swaggering gangster too smart for the law to catch up with, his shady financial backer, along with the power-hungry demagogues of the New and Old Left. Hearings against these men—and also from them—would be conducted not in secret, but in the full glare of publicity. Decisions to be handed down would be subject to no appeal other than that of majority public opinion.

There could be no good reason why governments, which owe their existence to the free choice of the population, should not, in times of peril, avail themselves of the identical means of self-preservation that less popular governments have all the time found serviceable. Should they, through tying themselves too closely to a paralyzing and crippling ideal of perfection, fail to act with sufficient vigor while it still lies within their ability to do so, they might well meet with the fate that once overtook the altogether too pure democracies that fell before Lenin and Hitler and Mussolini.

A mere handful of individuals of demoniacal proportions were during the early part of this century, and since, responsible for bringing upon the human race immense carnage and affliction. There were times when Lenin and Trotsky, Hitler and Goering, along with a busload or two of their henchmen, could have been apprehended; and then rendered harmless in one way or another. This was not done; and possibly for the good enough reason that they would at once have been freed by some high-minded judges, appalled at such invasion of constitutional rights.

Consider this question. How would the world have fared had a Committee of Public Order been set afoot in the summer of 1917 by the Russian Parliament, or in 1930 by the German Reichstag? For several dozen leading Bolsheviks or Nazis it would certainly have resulted in a very hard time. At the very least, they would no longer have been allowed to climb upon platforms and wooden crates to command attentive audiences. But on front porches, before kitchen stoves, in the presence of beer mugs and samovars, their frustrated admirers would have remained entirely free to growl their disapproval of the way things were being run, and to bemoan the fate of their idols; and no police need have rounded them up. Had Lenin,

Trotsky, Hitler and only a few other noteworthy agitators been permitted to suffer martyrdom, it is almost certain that all would have departed from the world without creating any great stir. Contrary to a widespread impression, martyrs differ from heroes, and are not as a rule to be too much concerned about. Doubtless, to the sociologists and kindred intellectuals of that period, any infringement of the civil and constitutional rights even of demagogues would have been considered unrighteous. But such anguish on their part would have been a small price to pay for the concentration camps that would not have been staked out, for the hideous deeds that would not have been performed within them, and for the oceans of blood that might not have been shed.

On the preceding matter I recommend to the attention of my readers a quotation from a distinguished man of letters of the nineteenth century, Thomas Babington Macaulay: "That, in great emergencies, the state may justifiably pass a retrospective act against an offender, we have no doubt whatever. We are acquainted with only one argument on the other side, which has in it enough reason to bear an answer. Warning, it is said, is the end of punishment. But punishment inflicted, not by a general rule, but by an arbitrary discretion, cannot serve the purpose of warning. It is therefore useless; and useless pain ought not to be inflicted. This sophism has found its way into several books on penal legislation. It admits, however, of a very simple refutation. In the first place, punishments *ex post facto* are not altogether useless even as warnings. They are warnings to a particular class which stand in great need of warnings. They remind persons of this description that there may be a day of reckoning for those who enslave and ruin their country in all forms of the law. But this is not all. Warning is in ordinary cases the principal end of punishment; but it is not the only end. To remove the offender, to preserve society from those dangers which are to be apprehended from his incorrigible depravity is often one of the ends."[14]

[14]Hallam, *Essays*

At the beginning of the present chapter reference was made to the question of majorities and minorities. That elected representatives should take it upon themselves to thwart the known wishes of a majority of their constituents is certainly not good. Yet how much more deplorable is it when the considered acts of popularly elected assemblies are habitually set at nought by fiat of nonrepresentative judicial bodies. For the arm of justice and orderly government thus to be stricken by a kind of paralysis in the name of a too ardent devotion to constitutional hairsplitting is now an everyday occurrence—a devotion, be it added, that is not unblended with ideological flavorings.

How long can such usurpation of authority on the part of men, who though learned and well meaning are responsible to no one, be assented to before the entire democratic process becomes dangerously compromised? All too possible is it for matters of far-reaching consequence to the security of the state to depend on the turn of a single vote. For this situation, a nonradical solution would have it that, other than by unanimous or near unanimous decision, no appellate court shall declare invalid or unconstitutional any act of Congress, Parliament, state or provincial legislature, or municipality.